THE GREAT PATH
OF AWAKENING

THE GREAT PATH
OF AWAKENING

AN EASILY ACCESSIBLE
INTRODUCTION FOR
ORDINARY PEOPLE

A COMMENTARY ON THE
MAHAYANA TEACHING
OF THE SEVEN POINTS
OF MIND TRAINING

Jamgon Kongtrul

Translated by KEN MCLEOD

SHAMBHALA
BOSTON & LONDON
2000

Shambhala Publications, Inc.
Horticultural Hall
300 Massachusetts Avenue
Boston, Massachusetts 02115
www.shambhala.com

Translation of *The Root Text of the Seven Points of Training the Mind* © 1981, 1986 by Chögyam Trungpa; revised translation © 1993 by Diana J. Mukpo and the Nālandā Translation Committee.

Printed in the United States of America
⊗ This edition is printed on acid-free paper that meets the American National Standards Institute Z39.48 Standard.
Distributed in the United States by Random House and in Canada by Random House of Canada Ltd.

Library of Congress Cataloging-in-Publication Data

Kon-sprul Blo-gros-mtha'-yas, 1813–1899.
  The great path of awakening.
  Translated from Tibetan.
  Bibliography: p.
  1. Mahayana Buddhism—Doctrines.   2. Spiritual life (Buddhism)
I. McLeod, Kenneth J.   II. Title.
BQ7402.K66   1987   294.3'4448   87-12775
ISBN 1-57062-587-5 (pbk.)

BVG 01

To my teacher, Kalu Rinpoche,
who originally gave me this book
and, with it, the opportunity
to help others

CONTENTS

PREFACE

IT IS MORE THAN TEN YEARS since the first translation
of this text was printed by Kalu Rinpoche's center in
Vancouver, Canada. Buddhism in the West has developed
considerably during that time. In particular, many people
have been introduced to this teaching and have had an
opportunity to practice it. Despite the many shortcomings in my original translation, Kongtrul's work has been
the focus of study and interest for many students of the
dharma. Other works on this topic—*Advice from a Spiritual Friend*, for instance—have also appeared.

In 1979, a French translation of the English text was
proposed. Well aware by then of the numerous corrections and improvements that should be made, I took that
opportunity to revise the original translation and expand
the footnotes. This new translation was subsequently
published by Kagyu Ling in France under the title
L'alchemie de souffrance. Circumstances prevented me then
from preparing a proper English manuscript for pub-
lication. Thanks largely to the kindness of Rick Rova and
Sue Forster, this essentially new translation is now complete. Many new resources were available for this translation that were not available before. In particular, the
Vidyadhara, Chögyam Trungpa, Rinpoche, has taught
extensively on this subject, and his comments and explanations have been extremely helpful.

A few of the changes warrant explanation. The
original English title was *The Direct Path to Enlighten-*

ment. Trungpa Rinpoche noted that this rendering was somewhat misleading in that the Tibetan indicated a main road or highway rather than a shortcut. The present title, it is hoped, reflects that idea more accurately. Further, in the previous edition, "The Seven Points" were originally attributed to Atisha. It is possible that all or parts of the text that Chekawa composed came from Atisha. Yet there is little direct evidence to justify that attribution and some evidence (for example, the dialect in which it is written) to suggest that it was principally Chekawa's composition. What is clear, however, is the importance that Atisha placed on this method as well as the wonderful power in his transmission of these teachings.

With respect to the translation itself, every attempt has been made to render the text in natural English rather than transposed Tibetan. Much of the latter part of the book (points six and seven) are written in a Tibetan dialect. I am grateful to Cyrus Stearns, who has been working with Dezhung Rinpoche, for giving me the benefit of his research on these phrases. Written as they are in idiomatic Tibetan, I have attempted to translate them into idiomatic English. Trungpa Rinpoche's own rendering has also been helpful and has been included in the Appendix for comparison.

Finally, I would like to thank Jane Gray, Tom Quinn, Eric Lawton, and others for their assistance in editing and improving the text.

KEN MCLEOD
Los Angeles, 1987

TRANSLATOR'S INTRODUCTION

IN THE ELEVENTH CENTURY, Buddhism in Tibet was reestablishing itself in the wake of the attempted suppression by Langdarma.[1] It was a time of intense interest in the Buddha's teachings. Numerous Tibetans undertook the long and hazardous journey to India to study with Buddhist masters, and Tibetan kings and rulers invited Indian masters to Tibet. Among those invited was Atisha,[2] one of the leading teachers of his day. Rinchen Zangpo, known as the Great Translator, had repeatedly urged him to come, both on his own initiative and as a representative of kings in western Tibet. In 1042, Atisha finally accepted the invitation.

In Tibet, Atisha worked to establish a proper perspective and understanding for spiritual practice by teaching a synthesis of three lineages of Indian Buddhism: the lineage of Profound Philosophy, which originated with Shakyamuni Buddha and was taught by Nagarjuna[3] through the inspiration of the bodhisattva Manjugosha;[4] the lineage of Vast Activity, which came from Shakyamuni Buddha and was taught by Asanga[5] through the inspiration of Maitreya;[6] and the lineage of Blessing and Practice from Buddha Vajradhara,[7] transmitted by Tilopa.[8] Particularly crucial in Atisha's presentation were the roles of refuge[9] and bodhicitta.[10] His insistence on refuge as the basis for all practice of dharma earned him the epithet "The Refuge Scholar."

Earlier in his life Atisha had experienced numerous visions and dreams that consistently pointed out the necessity of bodhicitta for the attainment of buddhahood. He was led to embark on a long sea journey to Indonesia to meet Serlingpa,[11] from whom he received the teachings of mind training in the mahayana tradition. In this system, one's way of experiencing situations in everyday life is transformed into the way a bodhisattva might experience those situations. Serlingpa himself composed texts on this method, one of which is included in the work translated here. Atisha gave these teachings to his closest disciple, Drom-tön Rinpoche,[12] the founder of the Kadampa[13] lineage. They were not taught widely at first and became generally known only with the Kadampa master Chekawa Yeshe Dorje[14] (1102–1176). Chekawa had come across them quite by accident. During a visit to a friend, he caught sight of an open book on a bed and read these lines:

> Give all victory to others;
> Take defeat for yourself.

Intrigued by this unfamiliar idea, he sought out the author and learned that the lines he had read came from *Eight Verses of Mind Traninig*[15] by Langri-tangpa (1054–1123). Although Langri-tangpa had already died, Chekawa was able to find Sharawa, another Kadampa teacher, who had also received this transmission. For twelve years, Chekawa studied and practiced mind training and summarized the teachings in *The Seven Points of Mind Training*. In later years, these teachings spread widely, and many teachers were inspired or urged by their students to write further on this subject.

Jamgon Kongtrul (1813–1899) was one of these teachers. As one of the principals of the nineteenth-century religious renewal in eastern Tibet, he likely welcomed the opportunity to write on a highly regarded teaching that had, by his time, been assimilated by all schools of Buddhism in Tibet.

Kongtrul was born and raised in the Bön[16] tradition. At an early age, he had acquired a thorough knowledge of this religion from his father, who was a Bön priest. Swept up by the political disturbances in his home country, Kongtrul found his way in his late teens into the Kagyupa[17] monastery of Pepung in eastern Tibet. His brilliance attracted the attention of Situ Pema Nyinje, the senior Kagyupa teacher at Pepung. Under his tutelage, Kongtrul progressed rapidly both spiritually and intellectually to become a teacher of note by his mid-twenties. His subsequent influence on Buddhism was enormous.

The text translated here is from the *gDams.ngag. mdsod*, a collection of teachings compiled by Kongtrul that presents the principal practices of each of the Tibetan schools of Buddhism. This collection is one of the five major works that Kongtrul produced. Known as *The Five Treasuries*, these works embrace all Tibetan learning and constitute one of the greatest contributions of the religious revival in eastern Tibet, the Ri-me movement.

This movement was initiated by a number of nineteenth-century teachers: Kongtrul, Khyentse Wangpo, Dza Patrul, Chok-gyur Lingpa, and others. These teachers had a number of objectives in mind, the three most important being to preserve rare teachings, to discourage sectarian prejudice, and to reemphasize practice and the application of dharma in everyday life.

The transmission of rare and little-known methods of practice is particularly vulnerable to interruptions. Since a broken transmission lineage cannot be restored, one concern of these teachers was to collect rare and effective meditation techniques that were in danger of being lost. This aim was realized principally through Kongtrul's and Khyentse's massive collections of contemplative techniques and their associated empowerments.

While Kongtrul and others wished to discourage rigid sectarianism, they had no intention of creating a new school or lineage. The Ri-me idea was one of a practice based on the lineage or teachings found most suitable by an individual accompanied by an appreciation of the quality and validity of all Buddhist traditions.

The third and perhaps most important concern was to reemphasize the application of dharma to everyday life. For these teachers, dharma could not be allowed to calcify into mere rote learning or chanting, a system of set responses and practices, but should lead individuals to the employment of intelligence and compassion in every aspect of their lives.

This theme is exactly the subject of *The Seven Points of Mind Training*. It is difficult for most of us to employ true intelligence and compassion in all circumstances. Our own interests, our own concerns for ourselves, constantly cloud and condition our perceptions of and responses to events around us. When our clinging to self is strong, we do not surrender it easily or willingly, and our attempts to use compassion and intelligence are clumsy and cause us regret or guilt. If, however, we understand that ego is a sham, that the self we cling to is in fact nothing, and we become familiar with the habit of letting go of our own interests in a situation, we become more capable of surrendering ego, just as we are able to throw away without regret an old sweater that never fit us anyway. This understanding and familiarization are developed in the sitting meditation that employs the techniques discussed in this work. Sitting meditation is essential, for it is the only method by which this approach to the world can be developed. Yet, if our day-to-day actions do not reflect our practice, our meditation is not effective: that is, not only should we become more tolerant, less arrogant, more open and responsive, but also we should feel genuinely at peace with ourselves, naturally happy and cheerful even in difficult situations, and our actions should not cause us regret or shame. Consequently, a major part of the book consists of guidelines for meeting ordinary situations in life. Continual practice of meditation and attention to everyday conduct go together—they are two aspects of practice rather than two unrelated activities. For instance, people whose training in this technique is well developed will, whenever they encounter someone who is troubled or in pain, spontaneously imagine that they take on the suffering of that person. When we work with both aspects, the habits of ego-clinging fall away, and true intelligence and compassion, the realization of nonself and nonreferential compassion, will arise.

The Great Path
of Awakening

Guru Buddha Bodhisattva Bhyonama[18]

> With undivided faith, I place upon my head
> The lotus feet of the Perfect Sage,
> Who first set in motion the wheel of love
> And triumphed completely in the two aims.[19]

> To the renowned sons of the Victorious One I
>   bow,
> To Manjushri, Avalokiteshvara, and the
>   others[20]
> Who set out in the ship of courageous
>   compassion
> And now liberate beings from the ocean of
>   suffering.

> The spiritual friend unsurpassable
> Reveals the noble path of compassion and
>   emptiness.
> He is the guide of all victorious ones.
> I prostrate myself at my guru's feet.

> I shall explain here the one path
> On which the Victorious One and his children
>   have traveled.

Easy to understand, it is not corrupted.
Easy to practice, it is entered with enthusiasm.
Yet it is profound, so buddhahood is attained.

In order to present a commentary on *The Seven Points of Mind Training*, which are particularly excellent pith instructions for cultivating bodhicitta, I shall discuss three topics: the source of this transmission, the need for this training, and the actual instructions.

The Source of the Transmission

THE GREAT AND GLORIOUS LORD ATISHA studied for lengthy periods under three great masters: Dharmakirti,[21] a master of bodhicitta who had received this oral transmission of the pith instructions of the mighty Sage and his sons; Guru Dharmarakshita,[22] who realized emptiness by relying on love and compassion and actually gave away some of his own flesh in an act of generosity; and Yogin Maitreya,[23] who really could take the sufferings of others onto himself. With tremendous diligence, Atisha carried his studies to completion, and bodhicitta filled his mind. He came to Tibet as a lord of the dharma. Although he had innumerable teachings that he could have presented, he chose to present only the methods that are discussed here. Of limitless numbers of students of the three kinds[24] whom he established in enlightenment and freedom, his three principal disciples were Ku-tön Tsön-dru, Ngo Lek-pe Sherab, and Drom-tön Gyal-we Jung-ne.[25] Drom-tön Rinpoche was held to be Avalokiteshvara, the embodiment of awakened compassion. Three traditions of teaching originate with him and his three principal disciples, emanations of the lords of the three buddha families:[26] the Canonical Texts, the Key Instructions, and the Pith Instructions.[27]

These teachings were transmitted by a succession of great spiritual teachers. The tradition of the exposition of the Six Canonical Texts of the Kadampas fell to the Gelukpa;[28] the presentation of the Key Instructions on the Four Truths[29] fell to the Dakpo Kagyu;[30] and both schools preserved the teachings of the Pith Instructions on the Sixteen Essences. The renowned Kadampa tradition holds the teachings of the Seven Dharmas and Deities: the four deities that adorn the body;[31] the three containers that adorn speech;[32] and the three disciplines that adorn mind.[33] Although this precious tradition contains limitless instructions that stand firmly in the sutra tradition yet have some connection with the tantra tradition,[34] they all definitely show only the path of joining compassion and emptiness. Since the specialization of this teaching is principally in the area of relative bodhicitta, the majority of notable individuals who have held this transmission have skillfully presented instructions for exchanging oneself with others and their success with them. From among the many different traditions of commentaries on this technique, *The Seven Points* explained here come from the tradition of spiritual instruction of Chekawa Yeshe Dorje.

The Need for Mind Training

DON'T EVEN CONSIDER the ephemeral happiness that results from birth in the higher realms[35] of gods and men. Although the enlightenment of shravakas and pratyekabuddhas[36] can be realized, it is not a final nirvana or transcendence of misery[37]. Consequently, we should strive only for the state of completely perfected buddhahood.[38] There are no methods to effect this attainment other than those which rely on two forms of meditation: relative bodhicitta, which is training the mind in love and compassion, and ultimate bodhicitta, which is resting evenly in a nondiscursive state free from conceptual elaborations. Nagarjuna says:

> If the rest of humanity and I
> Wish to attain insurpassable awakening,
> The basis for this is bodhicitta
> As stable as the King of Mountains:[39]
> Compassion, which touches everything,
> And pristine wisdom, which does not rely on
>   duality.

Moreover, whatever accumulations of merit and wisdom we may have, the root of spiritual development in the mahayana,[40] the six perfections, nonabiding nirvana,[41] and so on, is simply the arousal of bodhicitta. It arises on the basis of love and compassion. Even when full buddhahood is attained, there is nothing to do except to work for the welfare of others with nonreferential compassion. True ultimate bodhicitta will not arise in the course of experience of beginners, but relative bodhicitta will definitely arise if they train in it. With the development of relative bodhicitta, ultimate bodhicitta will be realized naturally.

So, for these and many similar reasons, we must meditate energetically on relative bodhicitta at the beginning if we are to achieve any meaningful results with respect to bodhicitta. For someone who wishes instruction on this subject, the basic method for training is, as Shantideva[42] says:

> He who desires shelter quickly
> For himself and for all others
> Should use this sacred mystery,
> The exchanging of oneself for others.

Consequently, only the method of meditation of exchanging oneself for others is explained in what follows. All other methods of mind training are simply elaborations of this theme.

The Actual Instructions

THE THIRD SECTION is divided into two parts: the actual explanation of the teachings of this tradition and additional instructions from the transmission lineage.

THE EXPLANATION OF THE SEVEN POINTS OF MIND TRAINING

The seven points are:

1. The preliminaries, which teach the support for dharma
2. The actual practice, training in bodhicitta
3. The transformation of adverse conditions into the path of awakening
4. The utilization of the practice in one's whole life
5. The extent of proficiency in mind training
6. Commitments of mind training
7. Guidelines for mind training

THE PRELIMINARIES, WHICH TEACH THE SUPPORT FOR DHARMA

As to the first point, the root text gives:

«*First, train in the preliminaries.*»

There are two points here, the preliminary to a period of meditation and preliminary instruction.

Preliminaries to a Period of Meditation

First, at the beginning of every period of meditation, imagine your root guru[43] sitting on a lotus-and-moon seat[44] above your head. His body is radiant and his face happy and smiling as he regards all beings with nonreferential compassion. In him, all the root and lineage gurus are present.[45]

With intense respect and devotion, repeat the lineage prayer[46] if you wish and, in particular, the following prayer a hundred or a thousand times.

> I pray for your blessing, my guru, great and
> completely worthy spiritual friend. I pray that
> you will cause love, compassion and bodhicitta
> to arise in my mind.

Then, imagine that your guru descends through the aperture of Brahma[47] and sits in your heart in a pavilion of light, like an open shell. This exercise in intense respect and devotion is known as guru yoga.[48] It is important to begin every period of meditation this way.

Preliminary Instruction

Second, with respect to preliminary instructions, if the four contemplations—that is, the difficulty of obtaining a free and well-favored existence, death and impermanence, consideration of the shortcomings of samsara,[49] and action as seed and result—are new to you, they are fully explained in the graded-path texts.[50] You need to work at these contemplations so that they definitely become part of your thinking. Here is a concise presentation of the basic points for those who would like one.

8

In order to obtain the framework for the practice of dharma, this precious human existence, which, in being free and well favored,[51] offers excellent opportunities, one must practice excellent virtue, since this is its karmic seed. Since the proportion of sentient beings that do practice virtue thoroughly is very small, the result, a free and well-favored existence, is difficult to obtain. When one considers the numbers of other sentient beings, such as animals, it is evident that human existence is just a remote possibility. Therefore, you should, above all else, work at dharma wholeheartedly so that the human existence now obtained is not wasted.

Furthermore, since life is uncertain, the causes of death are numerous, and one can't even be sure that death won't come today, one must exert oneself in the dharma right away. At the time of death, except for virtuous and nonvirtuous actions, nothing will follow, not wealth, food, possessions, nor land, body, or status. Since these are not even as helpful as a straw, there is not the slightest need for them.

After death, the power of karma[52] causes one to experience birth in one of the six classes of beings.[53] Whichever it is, there will be nothing but suffering, not even a strand of happiness.

Since happiness and suffering infallibly develop from virtuous and nonvirtuous actions, one should not do anything evil even at the risk of your life. One should practice only virtuous actions with great diligence.

You should energetically train yourself in this kind of thinking. At the end of every period of meditation, perform the seven-branch prayer[54] as many times as you are able to. In postmeditation periods, put the points of your reflections into practice. These instructions apply to all forms of preparation and actual practice.

THE ACTUAL PRACTICE: TRAINING IN BODHICITTA

As for the second point, there are two sections in the actual practice: the associated meditation on ultimate bodhicitta and the principal meditation on relative bodhicitta.

Ultimate Bodhicitta

The first section is again divided into two topics: instruction for a period of meditation and instructions for postmeditation practice.

MEDITATION

With respect to the first topic, after the practice of guru yoga described above, you should sit with the body straight and, as you breathe in and out, count without disturbance twenty-one breaths over and over again. This exercise will render you a suitable vessel for meditation practice. For the actual practice:

« Regard all phenomena as dreams. »

Actual phenomena—that is, the world and its inhabitants—are objects that we grasp at with our senses. These appearances are simply our mind's manifestations of confusion. In the end, they are not actually existent[55] in any way whatsoever, but are like the appearances in a dream. By thinking along these lines, train yourself to have some feeling for looking at the world this way.

Should you wonder if mind in itself[56] is real,

« Examine the nature of unborn awareness. »

When you look directly at the presence of mind, no color, no shape, no form is perceived. Since mind has no origin, it has never come into existence in the first place. Now it is not located anywhere, inside or outside the body. Finally, the mind is not some object that goes somewhere or ceases to exist. By examining and investigating mind, you should come to a precise and certain understanding of the nature of this awareness, which has no origin, location, or cessation.

Thoughts about this remedy for the tendency to cling to existence may come up. For example, you may think, "Mind and body all are empty" or "Nothing is helpful or harmful in emptiness." If this happens, then

«Even the remedy is freed to subside naturally.»

When you look at the presence of the remedy itself, these thoughts about the absence of true existence, there is nothing for mind to refer to and they subside naturally on their own. Relax in this state.

These lines present the key instructions on the meaning of existence from the point of view of investigative meditation.

«Rest in the nature of all, the basis of everything.»

This instruction presents the actual method of placing the mind. When there is no involvement with the activity of the seven groups of consciousness,[57] there is still the nature of all phenomena, the natural state, which is the basis of everything.[58] It is pointed out by the term "noble buddha-nature." Let go and rest, without the slightest idea of a nature existing as something, with absolutely no mental clinging, in a state distinguished by nondiscursive clarity and pure simplicity. In summary, for as long as you are able, follow no train of thought, but rest evenly in a state in which mind in itself is clear and free of discursiveness. This is placing meditation. Then, complete the period of practice with the seven-branch prayer as before.

POSTMEDITATION

The instruction for postmeditation practice is:

«In postmeditation practice, be a child of illusion.»

After meditation, do not allow the experience of resting evenly to dissipate, no matter what form of activity you engage in. Continually foster the feeling of knowing that all appearances, yourself, others, animate or inanimate, appear though they seem to be nothing[59]—be like a child of illusion.[60]

Relative Bodhicitta

Second, meditation on relative bodhicitta is explained in three parts: teachings on the preparation, on the actual practice, and on postmeditation practice.

PREPARATION

First do the preliminary practice of guru yoga as it was described above. Then you should meditate on love and compassion. They form the basis for taking and sending. Start by imagining that your own mother[61] is present in front of you. Think about her carefully with such reflections on compassion as these:

> This person, my mother, has looked after me with great effort right from the moment I was conceived in her womb. Because she endured all the hardships of illness, cold, hunger, and others, because she gave me food and clothing and wiped away my filth, and because she taught me what is good and steered me away from evil, I met the teachings of Buddha and am now practicing the dharma. What tremendous kindness! Not only in this life but in an infinite series of lives she has done exactly the

same thing. While she has worked for my welfare, she herself wanders in samsara and experiences many different forms of suffering.

Then, when some real compassion, not just lip service, has been developed and instilled, learn to extend it step by step:

> From time without beginning, each sentient being has been a mother to me in just the same way as my present mother. Each and every one has helped me.

With this sort of reflection, first meditate on objects for which it is easy to generate compassion: friends, spouse, relatives, and assistants, those in the lower realms where suffering is intense, the poor and destitute, and those who, though happy in this life, are so evil that they will experience the hell realms as soon as they die. When compassion in these areas has been instilled, meditate on more difficult objects: enemies, people who hurt you, demons, and others. Then meditate on all sentient beings, thinking along these lines:

> All these, my parents, not only experience many different kinds of suffering and frustration without intending to, but are also full of potent seeds for future suffering. How pitiable! What's to be done? To return their kindness, the least I can do is to help them by clearing away what hurts them and by making them comfortable and happy.

Train in this way until the feeling of compassion is intolerably intense.

MEDITATION
   Second,

   « Train in taking and sending alternately.
   Put them on the breath. »

As you think:

All these parents of mine, who are the focus of
compassion, are hurt directly by suffering and
indirectly by the source of suffering, so I shall
take on myself all the different kinds of suffering in all my mothers' course of experience and
the source of suffering, all disturbing emotions
and actions,[62]

meditate that all of this negativity comes to you and
foster a strong feeling of joy at the same time.
   As you think:

Without regret, I send all my virtuous activity
and happiness in the past, present, and future,
my wealth, and my body to all sentient beings,
my parents,

meditate that each individual receives all this happiness
and cultivate a strong feeling of joy in each one's receiving it.
   In order to make this imagined exchange clearer, as
you breathe in, imagine that black tar collecting all the
suffering, obscurations, and evil of all sentient beings
enters your own nostrils and is absorbed into your heart.
Think that all sentient beings are forever free of misery
and evil. As you breathe out, imagine that all your happiness and virtue pour out in the form of rays of moonlight
from your nostrils and are absorbed by every sentient

being. With great joy, think that all of them immediately attain buddhahood. To train the mind, use this practice of taking and sending with the breath as the actual practice for the period of meditation. Subsequently, always maintain the practice through mindfulness and continue to work with it. Shantideva, who has described this practice extensively, says:

> If I don't completely exchange
> My happiness for others' sorrow,
> Buddhahood will not be realized.
> There is no happiness in samsara.

POSTMEDITATION

Third, to apply this in postmeditation practice:

«*Three objects, three poisons, three seeds of virtue.*»

The three poisons continually arise in connection with three objects. Compulsive attachment arises for objects that are pleasant or useful; aversion arises for objects that are unpleasant or harmful; and stupidity or indifference for other objects. Recognize these poisons as soon as they arise. Then, for example, when attachment arises, think:

> May every bit of every sentient beings' attachment be contained in this attachment of mine. May all sentient beings have the seed of virtue of being free of attachment. May this attachment of mine contain all their disturbing emotions and, until they attain buddhahood, may they be free of such disturbing emotions.

Aversion and other emotions are used in practice by working with them the same way. Thus, the three poisons become three limitless seeds of virtue.

«Use sayings to train in all forms of activity.»

All the time, repeat these or other suitable sayings and cultivate these attitudes vigorously.

From Shantideva:

> While their evil ripens in me,
> May all my virtue ripen in them.

From the oral advice of the Kadampa tradition:

> I offer all gain and victory to the lords, all
>   sentient beings.
> I take all loss and defeat for myself.

From Gyal-se Tokme's[63] teachings:

> While all the suffering and evil of all sentient
>   beings ripens in me,
> May all my happiness and virtue ripen in
>   them.

«Begin the sequence of exchange with yourself.»

In order to be able to take on the sufferings of others, begin the sequence of exchange with yourself. Right now, take on mentally all the suffering that will ripen for you in the future. When that has been cleared away, take up all the sufferings of others.

THE TRANSFORMATION OF ADVERSE CONDITIONS INTO THE PATH OF AWAKENING

The third point concerns carrying practice into everyday life.[64]

«When evil fills the world and its inhabitants,
Change adverse conditions into the path of awakening.»

When your world is full of the pain and suffering that are the fruition of evil—when prosperity and wealth are diminishing, troublesome people create difficulties, and so on—you must change the adverse conditions in which you find yourself into the path of awakening. There are three ways to make this transformation: by relying on relative bodhicitta, on ultimate bodhicitta, and on special practices.

Relative Bodhicitta

For the first way:

«Drive all blame into one.»

Whether you are physically ill, troubled in your mind, insulted by others, or bothered by enemies and disputes, in short, whatever annoyance, major or minor, comes up in your life or affairs, do not lay the blame on anything else, thinking that such-and-such caused this or that problem. Rather, you should consider:

> This mind grasps at a self where there is no self. From time without beginning until now, it has, in following its own whims in samsara, perpetrated various nonvirtuous actions. All the sufferings I now experience are the results of those actions. No one else is to blame; this ego-cherishing attitude is to blame. I shall do whatever I can to subdue it.

Skillfully and vigorously direct all dharma at ego-clinging. As Shantideva writes in *Entering the Way of Awakening:*

17

What troubles there are in the world,
How much fear and suffering there is.
If all of these arise from ego-clinging,
What will this great demon do to me?

and

For hundreds of lives in samsara
He has caused me trouble.
Now I recollect all my grudges
And shall destroy you, you selfish mind.

«Be grateful to everyone.»

Work on taking and sending with these considerations in mind:

In general, all methods for attaining buddhahood rely on sentient beings. Therefore, to the
individual who wishes to awaken, sentient
beings are as worthy of gratitude as buddhas.
Specifically, all sentient beings are worthy of
gratitude since there is not one who has not
been my parent. In particular, all those who
hurt me are worthy of gratitude since they are
my companions and helpers for gathering the
accumulations of merit and pristine wisdom
and for clearing away the obscurations of disturbing emotions and conceptual knowledge.

Do not be angry, not even at a dog or an insect.
Strive to give whatever actual help you can. If you cannot
help, then think and say:

May this sentient being (or troublemaker)
quickly be rid of pain and enjoy happiness. May
he come to attain buddhahood.

Arouse bodhicitta:

From now on, all the virtuous acts I do shall be for his welfare.

When a god or a demon[65] troubles you, think:

This trouble now occurs because I, from time without beginning, have made trouble for him. Now I shall give him my flesh and blood in recompense.

Imagine the one who troubles you to be present in front of you and mentally give him your body as you say:

Here, revel in my flesh and blood and whatever else you want.

Meditate with complete conviction that this trouble-maker enjoys your flesh and blood, and is filled with pure happiness, and arouse the two kinds of bodhicitta in your mind.
Or:

Because I had let mindfulness and other remedies lapse, disturbing emotions arose without my noticing them. Since this troublemaker has now warned me of this, he is certainly an expression of my guru or a buddha. I'm very grateful to him because he has stimulated me to train in bodhicitta.

Or, when illness or suffering comes, think with complete sincerity:

If this hadn't happened, I would have been distracted by materialistic involvements and would not have maintained mindfulness of dharma. Since this has brought dharma to my attention again, it is the guru's or the Jewels' activity, and I am very grateful.

To sum up, whoever thinks and acts out of a concern to achieve his or her own well-being is a wordly person; whoever thinks and acts out of a concern to achieve the well-being of others is a dharma person. Langri-tangpa has said:

> I open to you as deep a teaching as there is. Pay attention! All faults are our own. All good qualities are the lords', sentient beings. The point here is: give gain and victory to others, take loss and defeat for ourselves. Other than this, there is nothing to understand.

Ultimate Bodhicitta
Second:

> *«To see confusion as the four kayas,*
> *The protection of emptiness is insurpassable.»*

In general all appearances, and particularly adverse conditions, are like the distress experienced when you dream of being burnt in a fire or swept away by a flood. The confused appearances of mind are invested with a reality that they do not have. It is rigorously established that, although these appearances arise, there is not even a particle of true existence[66] in them. When you rest in a state in which appearances simply arise but there is no clinging to them, the dharmakaya aspect is that they are empty in nature, the nirmanakaya aspect is they appear with clarity, the sambhogakaya aspect is that this emptiness and clarity occur together, and the svabhavikakaya aspect is that these are inseparable.[67] This key instruction, to rest evenly without grasping at origin, location, or cessation, points out the four kayas. It is the armor of view, the protection circle of emptiness, and the supreme instruction that cuts off confusion.

Special Practices

As for the third approach,

«The four applications are the best method.»

The four applications are accumulating merit, confessing evil actions, giving torma[68] to gods and demons, and offering torma to dakinis and protectors.[69] These are the best of all methods for using adverse conditions as a path.

ACCUMULATING MERIT

For the first, you should consider:

I wish to be happy, but suffering and frustration are all that come. This fact reminds me to cease evil actions, which are the seeds of suffering, and to accumulate merit, the seed of comfort and happiness. I shall do so.

Then, gather merit to the best of your ability through physical, verbal, and mental activities such as offerings to your guru and the Three Jewels, service to the sangha, torma offerings to local spirits, offering candles, making clay reliquaries, prostrating yourself, circumambulating, taking refuge, arousing bodhicitta, and, particularly, using the seven-branch prayer and offering mandalas.[70] Pray to put an end to hope and fear:[71]

If it's better for me to be ill,
I pray for the blessing of illness.
If it's better for me to recover,
I pray for the blessing of recovery.
If it's better for me to die,
I pray for the blessing of death.

CONFESSING EVIL ACTIONS

Second, with the same considerations as in the previous section, practice the four forces properly. The force of repudiation is to regret evil actions that you have done. The force of turning away from faults is the resolve not to repeat such actions, even at the risk of life. The force of reliance is taking refuge in the Three Jewels and arousing bodhicitta. The force of full engagement with remedies is the use of prayers that put an end to hope and fear, and the practice of the six kinds of remedies: meditation on emptiness, repetition of mantras and dharanis,[72] the making of images, performing the seven-branch prayer and offering mandalas, the recitation of sutras, and the repetition of special purification mantras.

GIVING TORMA TO GODS AND DEMONS

Third, give torma to troublemakers and direct them to enlightening activity:

> It's very kind of you to chase after me in response to what I've done to you in the past and to bring this debt to my attention. I ask you to destroy me now. I ask you to make all the sufferings, unpleasantness, poverty, ruin, misery, and disease that sentient beings experience ripen in me. Make all sentient beings free from suffering.

If you are unable to do that, give the torma and command them:

> When I meditate on love, compassion, and taking and sending, I am doing as much as I can to help you both now and in the future. Don't obstruct me in the practice of dharma.

OFFERING TORMA TO DAKINIS AND PROTECTORS

Fourth, offer torma to the protectors and direct them to be active in calming disruptive conditions and establishing conditions conducive to the practice of dharma. In particular, use the prayers given above to put an end to hope and fear.

*«In order to take unexpected conditions
as the path,
Immediately join whatever you meet
with meditation.»*

When illness, demons, interruptions, or disturbing emotions come unexpectedly, or if you see someone else troubled by some unpleasant situation, think, "I shall just practice taking and sending." In all your virtuous thoughts and actions think:

May all sentient beings come to engage naturally in much greater dharma activity than this.

Do the same when you are happy and comfortable. If you have some evil thought or are forced to engage in some form of evil activity, think:

May every evil thought and action of every sentient being be gathered in this one.

In summary, maintain the motivation to help others whatever you are doing: eating, sleeping, walking, or sitting. As soon as you encounter a situation, good or bad, work at this practice of mind training.

THE UTILIZATION OF THE PRACTICE IN ONE'S WHOLE LIFE

The fourth point, to teach a summary of practice for one's whole life, has two sections: what to do during one's life and what to do at death.

What to Do during One's Life

As to the first section:

«A summary of the essential instructions: Train in the five forces.»

The five forces summarize the crucial points of practice and, in a single phrase, contain numerous profound key instructions for the practice of the holy dharma. First is the force of impetus, to give a strong impetus to the mind by thinking:

> From this moment until enlightenment, at least from now until I die, and especially for the next year and the next month, and definitely from today until tomorrow, the two aspects of bodhicitta will never be absent from my mind.

The second is the force of familiarization. Whatever occupation or activity you are engaged in—virtuous, nonvirtuous, or indeterminate—maintain mindfulness and awareness strictly and train again and again in keeping the two aspects of bodhicitta ever in mind. In a word, study and train in bodhicitta as your principal form of virtuous activity.

The third is the force of virtuous seeds. Always concentrate your full energy—physical, verbal, and mental—on virtuous activity. Never be content with your efforts to arouse and strengthen bodhicitta.

The fourth is the force of repudiation. Whenever ego-cherishing thoughts come up, abandon them completely by thinking:

> Previously, for time without beginning, you have made me wander in samsara and experience different kinds of suffering. In addition, all the suffering and evil that occur in this life are brought on by you. There is no happiness in your company, so I shall now do everything I can to subdue and destroy you.

The fifth is the force of aspiration. At the end of any virtuous activity, pray sincerely and dedicate all virtue to these objectives:

> May I, on my own, guide all sentient beings to buddhahood. In particular, from now until I attain enlightenment, may I never forget the two aspects of precious bodhicitta, even when I am dreaming. May the two aspects of bodhicitta grow stronger and stronger. Whatever adverse conditions I encounter, may I take them as aids to bodhicitta.

What to Do at Death

Second, what are the instructions for the moment of death in this tradition of teaching?

> *« The mahayana instructions for how to die*
> *Are the five forces. How you act is important.»*

When a person who has trained in this teaching is stricken by terminal illness, he or she should practice the five forces. First, the force of virtuous seeds means to give away all possessions without a trace of attachment, clinging, or concern. In general, they can be given to one's gurus or to the Jewels. In particular, they can be given wherever the person thinks they will be most helpful. The force of aspiration means to make enlightenment the single focus of aspiration by practicing the seven-branch prayer if possible or, if not possible, by praying:

> Through the power of whatever virtuous seeds
> I have gathered in the three times, may I never
> forget but train and strengthen precious bodhi-
> citta in all future experiences in existence. May I
> meet the pure gurus who reveal this teaching. I

pray that these aspirations be realized through the blessing of my gurus and the Jewels.

The force of repudiation is to think:

This ego-cherishing has led me to suffer for countless existences, and now I experience the suffering of dying. Ultimately, there is nothing that dies, since neither self nor mind have true existence. I'll do whatever I must to destroy you, ego-clinging, who constantly think in terms of "I'm ill, I'm dying."

The force of impetus is to think:

I will never be without the two kinds of precious bodhicitta, not at death, nor in the intermediate state, nor in any future existence.

The force of familiarization is to bring clearly to mind the two bodhicittas that have been practiced previously.

While the main point is to practice these forces single-mindedly, the accompanying actions are also important. Physically, one should sit in the seven-point posture[73] or, if unable to do that, lie down on the right side and rest the cheek on the right hand while blocking the right nostril with the little finger. While breathing through the left nostril, one should begin by meditating on love and compassion and then train in sending and taking, in conjunction with the coming and going of the breath. Then, without clinging mentally to anything, one should rest evenly in a state of knowing that birth and death, samsara and nirvana, and so on, are all projections of mind, and that mind itself does not exist as anything. In this state, one should continue to breathe as well as one can.

There are many highly regarded instructions on how

to die, but none, it is said, is more wonderful than this one.

An instruction for death that employs a salve states: Apply to the crown of the head an ointment compounded of wild honey, ash from burning unspoiled seashells, and filings from an iron magnet.

THE EXTENT OF PROFICIENCY IN MIND TRAINING

The fifth point teaches the extent of proficiency in mind training.

«All dharma has a single purpose.»

Since the purpose of all dharma, both mahayana and hinayana, is simply to tame ego-clinging, as you practice dharma or work at mind training, ego-clinging should decrease. If your efforts in dharma do not counteract ego-clinging, your practice is meaningless. Since this is the one criterion that determines whether dharma practice is effective or not, it is said to be the yardstick by which a dharma person is measured.

«Of the two judges, rely on the principal one.»

For other people to see you as a dharma person is one judge, but ordinary people do not know what is hidden in your mind and may just be taking joy in certain improvements in the way you act. One sign of proficiency in mind training is that there is never any shame or embarrassment about your state of mind. Consequently, do not be attached to the judgment of others, but rely principally on the judge of mind itself.

«Always have the support of a joyful mind.»

When there is never any fear or despair no matter what adversity or suffering is encountered, when difficulty is taken as an aid to mind training and you always have the help of a joyful mind, then you have acquired proficiency in mind training. When adverse conditions come, meditate joyfully and, in addition, learn to take joyfully all the adversity others experience.

«You are proficient if you can practice even when distracted.»

A skilled horseman does not fall from his horse, even when he is distracted. In the same way, if you are able to take adverse conditions that suddenly develop as aids to mind training even without expressly directing your attention to do so, then you are proficient in mind training. The two bodhicittas arise clearly and effortlessly along with everything that appears—enemies, friends, troublemakers, happiness, or suffering.

These four lines describe signs that your training in bodhicitta has been effective and that proficiency has developed. They are not signs that you need not train further. Until buddhahood is attained, you should train to strengthen bodhicitta.

COMMITMENTS OF MIND TRAINING

The sixth point concerns the commitments of mind training.

«Always practice the three general principles.»

Of the three general principles, the first is not to break the promises you have made in mind training, that is, not to be tarnished by any fault or failing in any vow you have taken, including even the most minor precepts of individual liberation, bodhisattva, or vajrayana ordinations.[74]

The second principle is not to act scandalously, that is, to refrain from scandalous acts[75] such as destroying shrines, disturbing trees and other plants, polluting streams or rivers, associating with lepers and beggars, and other ways you might behave in the hope that others will think that you have no ego-clinging. Instead, make your way of life and practice utterly pure and faultless.

The third principle is to avoid being one-sided. For instance, although you may be patient with the trouble people cause, you may not be patient with the trouble caused by gods or demons, or vice versa. Or you may be able to handle those situations but be impatient with such sufferings as illness or disease. Maybe you can be patient in all sorts of difficult situations but let your practice of dharma lapse when you are happy and comfortable. The commitment is to avoid any bias or one-sidedness in mind training, so always practice that.

«Change your attitude, but remain natural.»

To change and reverse your previous attitude of concern with your own welfare and lack of concern for the welfare of others, take only the welfare of others as being important. Since all mind training should be practiced with little fanfare but great effectiveness, remain as natural as possible, keeping your manners and conduct like those of your friends and associates in dharma. Work at maturing your own experience without making others aware of your efforts.

«Do not talk about weak points.»

Don't discuss unpleasant subjects: other people's faults in wordly matters (such as physical or mental disabilities) or their faults in spiritual matters (violations of ordination, for instance). Talk cheerfully about pleasant topics in a gentle and friendly manner.

«Don't think about the affairs of others.»

Do not think about other people's affairs: in general, the faults of any sentient being, but in particular, the faults of anyone who has entered the practice of dharma. Rather, think:

> Seeing this fault is due to the impurity in my own outlook. Such a fault is not in this person. I am like those people who saw faults in Buddha, the enlightened one.

Thus, terminate this faulty attitude in your own mind.

«Work on the stronger disturbing emotions first.»

Examine your personality to determine which disturbing emotions are strongest. Concentrate all dharma practice on them in the beginning, and subdue and clear them away.

«Give up all hope for results.»

Give up the hope of subduing gods and demons by meditating on mind training, or the hope that you will be considered a good person when you try to help someone who has hurt you. These are hypocritical attitudes. In a word, give up all hope for any result that concerns your own welfare, such as the desire for fame, respect, happiness, and comfort in this life, the happiness experienced in the human or god realms in future lives, or the attainment of nirvana for yourself.

«Give up poisonous food.»

Since all virtuous thoughts and actions motivated by clinging to a concrete reality or to a self-cherishing attitude are like poisonous food, give them up. Learn not to cling, but to know the phantomlike nature of experience.

«Don't rely on consistency.»

A person who is consistent in his affairs doesn't forget the people who concern him, no matter where he is or how much time has gone by. When someone causes you trouble and has made you angry, you might never let go of that resentment. Stop it. Take a helpful attitude or action in response to someone who causes trouble.

«Don't be excited by cutting remarks.»

In general, don't take joy in disparaging others. In particular, when another person says something bad about you, don't respond by talking maliciously about him to others. In fact, even if some injury has resulted, strive always to praise the good qualities of others without blaming this or that person.

«Don't wait in ambush.»

When someone has caused you trouble, the tendency is to fix it in mind and never forget it though many years go by. When there is an opportunity to ambush the person and to return the injury, revenge is taken. Give up this approach and be as helpful as you can in your response to troublesome situations. For the kind of trouble caused by demons, don't cling to the problem, but work only on love and compassion.

«Don't make things painful.»

Don't speak in a way that causes pain for others, either by making pointed remarks and exposing their faults or, in the case of nonhuman beings, by using mantras that drain their life.

«Don't put the horse's load on a pony.»

To give someone else an unpleasant job that is your responsibility or, by resorting to trickery, to shift a problem you have encountered to someone else is like putting a horse's load on a pony.[76] Don't do this.

«Don't aim to win.»

In a horse race, the aim is to be the fastest. Among dharma people there are often hopes of receiving more attention or being more highly regarded than others, and little schemes are made up to find ways to acquire possessions. Give these up. Have no concern about receiving or not receiving recognition or prestige.

«Don't revert to magic.»

If you accept a setback for the time being out of a desire for future benefits for yourself or if you practice mind training expecting to cure illness and mental disturbances and ward off adverse situations, your practice is mistaken, like someone contriving magical rituals. Don't act this way. Whatever happiness or sorrow comes, meditate without arrogance, hesitation, fear, or hope. Gyal-se

Tokme has said:

> Mind training done with that kind of attitude
> should be considered a method for helping de-
> mons and disturbances. If you practice that
> way, it's no different from evil. Dharma work
> must counteract discursive thought and dis-
> turbing emotions.

With this example, consider the topic of mistaken
dharma practice. Mistaken outlooks are outlooks based
on eternalism or nihilism; mistaken meditation is meditation that clings to some sublime state; mistaken conduct
is conduct that is not consistent with the three ordinations. Mistaken dharma denotes anything that is con-
tradictory to the ethics or outlook authoritatively taught
in the holy dharma, regardless of whom it comes from,
you or someone else, the very best or the very least. It
will propel you into samsara and the lower realms. It's
like taking the wrong medicine for an illness or applying
the wrong disciplinary measures.

There are individuals who call certain composed and
revealed works[77] "mistaken dharma" without examining
the words or thoughts in a single chapter to see whether
they are pure or mistaken. It would appear that they issue
their pronouncements out of attachment to their own
systems or from personal differences. It is said that no one
but a buddha is able to evaluate the worth of an individual. So, even though you may not like a person who
has arrived at a proper outlook and ethics, your dislike
doesn't make the dharma mistaken. For example, a merchant may sell gold or glitter, but it doesn't make him a
better or worse merchant. Buddha said over and over
again:

> Don't rely on individuals; rely on the dharma.

I make this digression here because it is so important to understand this point.

«*Don't reduce a god to a demon.*»

If, as you meditate on mind training, your personality becomes stiff with pride and arrogance, it's as though you have reduced a god to a demon; dharma has become nondharma. The more you meditate on mind training and dharma, the more supple your personality should become. Act as the lowest servant to everyone.

«*Don't seek pain as a component of happiness.*»

Don't think: "If that patron or person should become ill or die, I would receive a lot of food and money" [78] or "If this fellow monk or these dharma companions were to die, I would obtain their images and books" or "If my colleagues were to die, all the merit would come to me alone" or "Wouldn't it be wonderful if all my enemies were to die!"

In a word, you must refrain from hoping for suffering to come to others as a way of extending your own comfort and happiness.

GUIDELINES FOR MIND TRAINING

The seventh point presents guidelines for mind training.

«*All active meditation is done in one way.*»

Continue practice into everyday life with a single meditation, always keeping in mind the intention to help others in all activities, eating, dressing, sleeping, walking, or sitting.

« All corrections are made in one way.»

Analysis itself is used to correct mistakes in analysis. If, when you are meditating on mind training, adverse conditions develop, people criticize and insult you, demons, devils, enemies, and disputes trouble you, your disturbing emotions become stronger, or you have no desire to meditate, think:

> In the whole universe, there are many sentient beings who have problems like mine; my compassion goes out to all of them,

and:

> In addition to this unwanted situation, may all the unwanted circumstances and suffering of all sentient beings be collected here,

and use the single corrective of exchanging yourself for others.

« At the beginning and at the end,
Two things to be done.»

At the beginning, as soon as you wake up in the morning, generate very strongly the impetus:

> Today, I shall keep the two bodhicittas with me.

During the day, maintain them with continuous mindfulness. At the end, when you go to sleep in the evening, examine your thoughts and actions of the day. If there were infringements of bodhicitta, enumerate the instances and acknowledge them, and make a commitment that such will not occur in the future. If there have been no infringements, meditate joyfully and pray that you and all other beings may be able to engage in bodhicitta even more effectively in the future. Practice these two activities regularly. Take the same approach to any infringements or violations of ordination.

«Whichever of two occurs, be patient.»

If you become utterly destitute and are suffering greatly, consider your previous karma. Without being resentful or depressed, take up all the sufferings and evil of others and work hard at ways to clear away evil actions and obscurations. If you find yourself very happy and comfortable, surrounded by great wealth and servants, don't succumb to carelessness or indifference. Use the wealth for virtuous projects, use your power constructively, and pray for all sentient beings to have the same comfort and happiness. In short, whichever occurs, happiness or suffering, be patient.

«Observe these two, even at the risk of your life.»

Since all present and future happiness comes from carefully observing the general precepts of dharma contained in the three ordinations and the particular precepts of mind training with their corresponding commitments, observe both these sets of precepts even at the risk of your life. Moreover, whatever you do, observe them not from a concern and consideration for your own welfare but only with the intention of being helpful to others.

«Learn the three difficult points.»

At first, it is difficult to recognize disturbing emotions. Then, it is difficult to overcome them. In the end, it is difficult to cut their continuity. Therefore, you should train in these three points. First, recognize disturbing emotions for what they are as soon as they arise. Then, stop them by taking corrective measures. Finally, be decisive in your attitude that such disturbances will never arise again.

«Take up the three primary resources.»

The primary resources for working at dharma are a good guru, the proper practice of dharma with a workable mind, and suitable conditions for dharma practice—food, clothing, and so on. If these three are all available to you, take joy in that and pray that they be available to others, too. If they are not all available, meditate on compassion for others and take on yourself the deficiencies that all sentient beings experience in these primary resources. Pray that you and all others may have them.

«Don't allow three things to weaken.»

Learn not to let these three things weaken. Faith and respect for your guru must not weaken since all the fine qualities of mahayana dharma depend on him. Enthusiasm for meditation on mind training must not weaken since mind training is the very core of the mahayana. Observation of the precepts of the three ordinations must not weaken either.

«Make the three inseparable.»

Make the three faculties—body, speech, and mind —always inseparable from virtuous actions, and refrain from evil.

«Train in all areas without partiality. Overall deep and pervasive proficiency is important.»

Without partiality for certain areas, mind training by itself should pervade everything, good or bad, which arises as an object of experience: other sentient beings, the four elements, or nonhuman beings. Deeply trained proficiency, not just lip service, is important.

«Always meditate on volatile points.»

Meditate by skillfully bringing out extra love and compassion for subjects that present difficulties in mind training: aggressive enemies, troublesome obstacles, particularly those who act perversely and respond to your help by making trouble, people who compete with you, casual friends, people who are troublesome even though there is no bad feeling, or those with whom you just don't get along. In particular, avoid anything that will cause trouble with people with whom you have a close relationship—your guru or your parents, for instance.

«Don't depend on external conditions.»

Have no regard for conducive or adverse conditions, strong or weak health, wealth or poverty, good or bad reputation, troubles or absence of troubles. If conducive conditions come about, train the mind right then. If conducive conditions are not present, then work on the two bodhicittas right then. In a word, don't be concerned with your situation or other factors; never let go of your practice of mind training.

«This time, practice the important points.»

From time without beginning, you have taken existence in innumerable forms, in all of which nothing meaningful has been done. A similar coincidence of the conducive conditions in this life will not come about in the future. Now that you have obtained a human existence and met the pure dharma, you should put the main points into practice in order to realize objectives of permanent significance. So aims for future lives are more important than aims for this life. For the future, freedom is more important than samsara. The welfare of others is more important than your own. Of practicing and teaching the dharma, practicing is the more important. Training in bodhicitta is more important than other practices. Further, intensive meditation on your guru's instructions is more important than analytical meditation based on texts. Sitting on your mat and training are more important than other forms of activity.

«Don't make mistakes.»

Avoid six mistakes. To endure patiently the suffering of subduing enemies, protecting friends, and working to make money and not to endure patiently the difficulties of dharma practice is mistaken patience. To want wealth, happiness, and comfort in this life and to have no inclination to practice dharma thoroughly is mistaken inclination. To enjoy the taste of wealth and possessions and not to enjoy the taste of hearing, reflection, and meditation on the dharma is mistaken enjoyment. To have compassion for a person who puts up with hardship in order to practice dharma and not to have compassion for those who do evil is mistaken compassion. To engage people who look to you in bettering only their position in this life and not to engage them in dharma is mistaken care. To take joy in other people's unhappiness and in the sufferings of your enemies and not to take joy in virtue and happiness in nirvana or samsara is mistaken joy. Avoid these six mistakes completely.

«Don't fluctuate.»

A person who sometimes practices and sometimes doesn't has not developed a definite understanding of dharma. Don't have a lot of projects on your mind, but do mind training single-mindedly.

«Train wholeheartedly.»

Without indulging any distraction, train yourself only in mind training, being completely involved with this one concern.

«Find freedom through both examination and investigation.»

You must find freedom from disturbing emotions and ego-clinging by constantly examining and investigating your course of experience. Therefore, turn your attention to an object that gives rise to disturbing emotions. Examine carefully whether they arise or not. If they do arise, apply remedies vigorously. Again, look at ego-clinging to see what it is like. If it appears that no ego-clinging is present, examine it again in reference to an object of attachment or aversion. If ego-cherishing then arises, immediately stop it with the remedy of exchanging yourself for others.

«Don't make a fuss.»

Don't make a big fuss even when you are kind to another person, because you are, in fact, just working at regarding others as more important than yourself. Since all the time and hardship you put into being well educated, moral, and practicing the dharma benefit you, there is no point in making a fuss about it to others. Don't trade boasts with others. In the counsels of Ra-treng,[79] it says: "Don't expect much of people; pray to your yidam." [80]

«Don't be caught up in irritation.»

Don't take a jealous attitude toward others. When others disparage you in public or cause trouble for you, don't react or let your mind and feelings be disturbed. Potowa[81] said:

> Because all of us, though we are dharma persons, have not made dharma a remedy for ego-clinging, we are more sensitive than a newly healed wound. We are more caught up by irritations than Tsang-tsen.[82] This is not effective dharma. Dharma, to be effective, must remedy ego-clinging.

«Don't be temperamental.»

Don't trouble the minds of your companions by showing your pleasure or displeasure on every little matter.

«Don't expect thanks.»

Don't hope that others will express their gratitude in words of thanks for your own practice of dharma, your helping others, or your practicing virtue. In a word, get rid of any expectation of fame or prestige.

All these points of advice are means that will strengthen mind training and prevent it from weakening. In summary, Gyal-se Rinpoche[83] said:

> Throughout our lives we should train well in the two kinds of bodhicitta, using both meditation and postmeditation practices, and acquire the confidence of proficiency.

Make an effort to follow this instruction.

CONCLUDING VERSES

« This quintessential elixir of instruction,
Which changes the five kinds of degeneration
Into the way of awakening,
Is a transmission from Serlingpa.»

Since the five kinds of degeneration—the times, sentient beings, life, emotions, and outlook—are steadily advancing, happy situations conducive to dharma are few, and disruptive and adverse conditions proliferate. While the remedies in other teachings may not be effective, for someone who uses mind training, virtuous activity increases directly with the proliferation of adverse conditions, just as the flames of a fire become stronger and stronger as more and more wood is piled on. This teaching has a special feature that others lack. It changes all disturbing emotions and adverse conditions into the way of awakening. These instructions are like the quintessence of an elixir and will enrich the course of experience and be helpful to everyone whatever his or her capabilities. They are profound teachings transmitted from Lord Serlingpa, the very kindest of Lord Atisha's three principal gurus.

« The awakening of the karmic energy
of previous training
Aroused intense interest in me.
Therefore, I ignored suffering and criticism
And sought instruction for subduing ego-clinging.
Now, when I die, I'll regret nothing.»

When the karmic energy from the previous existences of the great spiritual teacher Chekawa was awakened, his only interest was this teaching. Through great hardships, he sought and received the root of all dharma, the key instructions for subduing ego-clinging, from the great father-son lineage of Atisha. When he had trained well in these methods, he cherished others more than himself, and never again did any concern for his own desires arise. Because he had acquired confidence through realizing the purpose of entering the dharma, he regretted nothing.

The last two verses above are the concluding comments of Chekawa, the author of this tradition of teaching.

ADDITIONAL INSTRUCTIONS FROM THE TRANSMISSION LINEAGE

The second section is a selection of additional instructions from the transmission lineage. This deep teaching on mind training is helpful if you are on your own. Mind training by itself is capable of bringing all happiness and suffering into practice. In addition, when profound dharma stirs up evil karma, your mind is also stirred up. When you are active, you want to sit still; when you sit still, you want to be active. If this kind of problem comes up, meditate in this way:

> When I am in this kind of mood
> My mat is by far the best place to be.
> This present mental state is fine.
> Moreover, by putting up with this
> unpleasantness,
> I won't be born in the hell realms. How
> wonderful!
> I won't be baked or roasted. How wonderful!

And:

Further, I should think well of fear and alarm
And have a healthy sense of shame,
Accept mean food and bear hardships,
Wear poor clothes and accept a low position,
Work at remedies, and disregard happiness
    and suffering.

According to these teachings from *The Stages of the Awakening Warrior*,[84] self-criticism should get to the point.

When you are ill, illness is the nurse. So, when you are agitated, thinking that your doctors, nurses, relatives, and others should try harder to cure you, think:

No one else is to blame for this illness; ego-clinging alone is responsible.

If medicine and nursing do help, to think that the right treatment wasn't tried earlier is to take the wrong attitude. Rather think:

No one is free from this kind of affliction. Now, ego-clinging, this is what you wanted, so be satisfied.

In addition, learn to take on the illness and disturbances that trouble others.

Here are some of Lord Serlingpa's teachings:[85]

Flatten all thoughts.
All remedies are weapons to strike with.
Concentrate all plans into one.
All paths have one goal.
These four teachings are enlightening
    remedies.
You will need them to subdue the uncivilized.
In these degenerate times, they are needed
    to cope with evil associates and mistaken
    practices.

As soon as thoughts arise, flatten them in mind training or emptiness. Remedies aren't just meditations to be used when it's convenient. As soon as disturbing emotions arise, jump on them, round them up, isolate and crush them.[86] Don't plan many different projects for the present or future. Concentrate only on what helps your mind and on doing the best you can to destroy ego-clinging. Since freedom from ego-clinging is buddhahood, this single goal is enough. There is no need to enumerate the stages on the path. These four teachings summarize all the remedies concerned with enlightenment.

> Adverse conditions are spiritual friends.
> Devils and demons are emanations of the
>   victorious ones.
> Illness is the broom for evil and obscurations.
> Suffering is the dance of what is.
> These four teachings are for really disruptive
>   emotions.
> You will need them to subdue the uncivilized.
> In these degenerate times, they are needed
>   to cope with evil associates and mistaken
>   practices.

You don't have to avoid adverse conditions, since they perform the function of a spiritual friend. By using adverse conditions, you can gather the accumulations, clear away obscurations, be reminded of dharma, and derive benefit from your understanding. There is no need to be frightened of visions and hallucinations associated with gods or devils or of the trouble that demons cause. Because they help to increase your faith and virtue, they are emanations of your guru or of buddhas. Since previous evil karma is stirred up when you practice the holy dharma properly, various physical illnesses come again and again. When this happens, work at being joyful when

45

ill, since it is repeatedly said in the sutras that even a slight headache, to say nothing of a serious illness, is like a broom sweeping away dust. Sickness clears away all the evil and obscurations gathered from time without beginning. When suffering comes, if you look at just what it is, it arises as emptiness. However much you suffer, the suffering is just the dance of what is, so you shouldn't be depressed. It's good if all these things happen, since they can be taken as aids to putting dharma into practice. Thus, the key point is not to avoid these four instructions for really disruptive emotions. Put them into practice.

> There's a great yoke for happiness.
> There's a great lift for suffering.
> The unwanted is the first wish.
> The worst portents are joyfully accepted.
> These four teachings are correctives for other
>   remedies.
> You will need them to subdue the uncivilized.
> In these degenerate times, they are needed
> To cope with evil associates and mistaken
>   practices.

When you are happy and comfortable in body and mind, the desire to do something not concerned with dharma comes up. When you look at just what this feeling of happiness is, there is nothing substantial to it. Take this situation into practice by giving this mere appearance of happiness to all sentient beings. Not to succumb to this appearance of happiness, just to rest in a natural state, is the yoke for happiness. When you are suffering, don't despair. When you look at just what it is, it disappears as being empty. In addition to the appearance of suffering, take on the suffering and unhappiness of all sentient beings and rest in a natural state. This practice is the lift for suffering. When everything you don't want or don't wish for descends on you, in being an aid to destroying ego-

clinging it is, in fact, your first wish, your first concern.
Let your mind rest happily at ease as you think:

> This is what you wanted, ego-clinging. May it
> completely destroy you.

When there are bad portents or when hallucinations
occur, you wonder a lot about what is happening and
what you should do. At such times, think:

> This had to happen. It's good that it has come
> up. May all bad portents be heaped on top of
> this ego-cherishing,

and rest without self-indulgence or hesitation. These four
teachings are correctives for situations other remedies
can't handle.

> Ego is the root of faults.
> This is a teaching to throw it out.
> Others are the source of fine qualities.
> This is a teaching to accept them completely.
> These two teachings summarize remedies.
> You will need them to subdue the uncivilized.
> In these degenerate times, they are needed
> To cope with evil associates and mistaken
>   practices.

To be brief, because the whole basis of mind training is contained in the two principles of throwing out
concern for your own welfare and taking complete hold
of the welfare of others, these teachings summarize this
course of instruction. For this reason, take it as the basis
for practice.

> Turn error right around and look right in.
> Relax completely and rest comfortably.
> Not being held, they will go freely.

If you follow any thought or emotion, major or minor, and let your mind wander outward, your work is in error and you're no different from an ordinary person. Turn your attention right in and look right at your mind. When you look at it, nothing is seen. Relax completely, let everything go, and rest in that state of emptiness. No matter how many thoughts or emotions there are, when they aren't held, they go freely on their own and become the accumulation of pristine wisdom. This instruction is the essence of meditation on ultimate bodhicitta.

Conclusion

THIS TRADITION of the seven points includes all the essential points of practice of every tradition of commentary that transmitted instructions for the mind-training practice coming from the oral tradition of Atisha. Of all the innumerable authors and their commentaries, detailed or brief, I have received precisely this interpretation from the written commentaries of the very noble Gyal-se Rinpoche Tokme and the noble and revered Kunga Nyingpo.[87] All the teachings given by notable persons have been gathered and distilled into a single elixir, which is presented here with the principal aim of being easily understood by beginners. Thus, this comprehensive and clarifying work was composed only with the noble intention to help others.

> The source of the path of sutras and tantras,
> The vital essence of all holy dharma,
> Profound yet easily practiced,
> Arises wonderfully from all instruction.
> It's difficult to hear deep teaching like this.
> It's difficult to apply it when heard.
> To act on this is to be rich in merit.
> It's as rare these days as gold found on the
>   ground.
> Now, too much talk is wearisome,
> But with the pure wish to help others
> I have written this text.
> By this virtue, may all beings
> Master the two bodhicittas.

At the long-standing urging of my student Karma
Tu-tob, who is well versed in the five fields of learning,
and at the more recent requests of the incarnate Karma Tabke Namrol, who has undertaken to hold closely
to bodhicitta with honest determination, and of Lama
Karma Nge-don and others who are worthy in their ad-
herence to practice, and in the face of consistent entreaties
by those who wished to clarify their practice, Lodru
Taye, a subject of the kind lords Karmapa and Situ, composed this work in the retreat center of the Clear Light
Park of Great Bliss and Total Goodness at Pepung Monastery. May infinite numbers of beings benefit.

May virtue grow strong.

NOTES

1. Langdarma (803–842). Buddhism was first established in Tibet in the seventh century by King Song-tsen-gampo. During his reign, the Tibetan language was provided with an alphabet by Tumi Sambhota, and translations of texts from Sanskrit to Tibetan began. Under the next king, Tri-song Detsen, Indian masters such as Shantarakshita, Padmasambhava, and Vimalakirti were invited. The monastic code was introduced, monasteries were built, and the work of translation continued on a large scale. Buddhism flourished under the two following kings, but when Langdarma came to the throne in 836, he instigated a ruthless suppression of Buddhism, closing monasteries, slaughtering monks, burning libraries, and destroying shrines and other religious objects. Although his reign ended in his assassination six years later, it left behind only the most tenuous thread of Buddhism in Tibet.

Langdarma's reign marks the division between the Old and New Translation schools: the Old School continued the tradition of Buddhism that was first introduced to Tibet and survived the persecution; the New School consisted of the traditions that were brought to Tibet after Langdarma's reign. Rinchen Zangpo is generally regarded as the first of the new generation of translators.

2. Atisha (982–1054). From the time Atisha was eight years old, he enjoyed a close relationship with the deity Green Tara, the embodiment of the activity of awakened compassion. By his early twenties, he was a proficient master of the esoteric teachings of Buddhism and a profound scholar whose skill in debate was highly valued in contests with representatives of other Indian religions. Both Tara, in his visions, and his own associates consistently urged him to become a monk in order

to help beings more effectively. Eventually acceding to this request, he became famous for the purity of his observance of the monastic code. He was one of the principal teachers at Vikramashila, one of the largest and most famous monastic universities of Buddhist India. He was also named the Holder of the Seat of Bodhgaya (the location of Buddha Shakyamuni's awakening), in recognition of his mastery and attainment.

Atisha's spiritual development is closely linked with the numerous visions he had of Green Tara. It was she who urged him to seek the teachings on bodhicitta. In addition, Atisha repeatedly had other visionary experiences that indicated the importance of this subject. On one occasion at Bodhgaya, two of the many statues that decorated the main temple spoke. One asked, "What is the most important teaching for attaining buddhahood?" The other replied, "Bodhicitta is the most important teaching." The end result was that Atisha jouneyed to Indonesia to study with Dharmakirti, whose understanding of bodhicitta and the ways to develop it were universally respected.

Later in his life, Atisha committed a serious fault by permitting an advanced practitioner of esoteric teachings to be expelled from a temple for seemingly inappropiate behavior. When Atisha consulted with Tara on the matter, she advised him to teach the dharma in Tibet to clear away the karmic residues of that action. Thus, with some reluctance, Atisha finally accepted Rinchen Zangpo's invitations.

Atisha spent the last twelve years of his life in Tibet, teaching from his vast knowledge of Buddhist philosophy and practice, assisting translators such as Rinchen Zangpo in their work of rendering faithfully the Sanskrit texts into Tibetan, and guiding students in their spiritual practice.

3. Nagarjuna: an Indian master who lived about the first century of the common era. Nagarjuna was one of the greatest dialecticians the world has known, and his works definitively established the "middle way" (*madhyamika*) between the dualistic extremes of origin and cessation, nihilism and eternalism, coming and going, monism and pluralism. A teacher at the famous monastic university of Nalanda, his expositions on emptiness and other topics of Buddhist philosophy are still

used today as authoritative guides for intellectual understanding and contemplative practice.

The name Nagarjuna means "he with power over the nagas"—the *naga* being a form of serpent. This epithet refers to his recovery of the Buddha's teachings on the Perfection of Wisdom from the naga-king who guarded them. Nagarjuna's commentaries on this profound teaching led to the formation of the tradition of Profound Philosophy, which establishes the intellectual understanding of emptiness as a basis for contemplation.

4. Manjugosha or Manjushri: the bodhisattva (see note 10) of awakened intelligence. He is usually depicted holding the flaming sword of compassion, which cuts through clinging to duality, and a volume of *The Perfection of Wisdom*, which he has taken completely to heart.

5. Asanga: a third-century Indian master who is regarded as the founder of the tradition of Vast Activity. This tradition emphasized the primacy of experience and the understanding of the false duality of subjective and objective existence.

Asanga is particularly known for his relationship with the bodhisattva Maitreya (see note 6). After twelve years of meditation and prayer to meet Maitreya, Asanga gave up and left his cave. He came across an old dog covered with sores that were infested with maggots. The sight aroused such pity in him that he sought to relieve the dog's suffering by removing the maggots—not with his finger, for fear of killing them, but with his tongue. As he extended his tongue and closed his eyes against the revolting sight, the dog disappeared and Asanga found himself licking the ground. When he opened his eyes, Maitreya was standing before him. Maitreya explained that it was only Asanga's obscurations that had prevented them from meeting. This compassionate act had removed the last obscurations, and Asanga could now see him. Maitreya then took Asanga to the Tushita Realm, where he taught him the mahayana teachings known as *The Five Teachings of Maitreya*.

6. Maitreya: the future buddha. Before descending from the Tushita Realm to appear in the world, Buddha Shakyamuni appointed Maitreya as his regent. The name Maitreya means

"one who possesses loving-kindness." He is usually depicted sitting in a chair teaching the dharma.

7. Vajradhara, the Holder of the Vajra: the expression of full awakening in the tantric tradition (see note 34) of Buddhism. The vajra is the weapon of Indra, the Indian counterpart of Zeus. It is made of indestructible material and can destroy any other object without being affected itself. As such, it is a symbol of the spiritual potential of every sentient being, which, unaffected by all the relative realities of existence, is indestructible and has the power to destroy all the fabrications that create suffering and misery. Vajradhara is one who wields the full power of spirituality, the awakening into buddhahood. Iconographically, Vajradhara is depicted as a blue figure (representing the sky, the unchanging nature of that which is ultimate) holding a vajra and a bell, which are expressions of intelligence and skill.

8. Tilopa (988–1069): an Indian master who received direct inspiration from Buddha Vajradhara. In the lineage of Blessing and Practice, great emphasis is placed on the role of the guru (see note 43), the inspiration and blessing that he transmits, and actual practice on the part of the student.

9. Refuge. In Buddhism, ordinary existence is viewed as being fraught with suffering, fear, misery, and pain, and the initial spiritual urge is expressed by the phrase "going for refuge." Refuge, then, implies an abandonment of allegiance to ordinary criteria of what is meaningful. In this state of questioning, one entertains the possibility of awakening and derives inspiration from the fact of the enlightenment of Shakyamuni Buddha. "Going for refuge" means orienting oneself toward the attainment of enlightenment—taking refuge in Buddha. In addition, one takes refuge in the dharma, the teachings and experience of awakening, and in the sangha, the teachers and other practitioners, who provide guidance and support on this path. These three—Buddha, dharma, and sangha—are known as the Three Jewels. From the point of view of Buddhism, an end to suffering and frustration can be found only through awakening to a true understanding of oneself and the world, but the path to that internal understanding requires expert guidance by someone who knows the way.

10. Bodhicitta. This term expresses the core of the mahayana teachings. Conventionally, it denotes both the aspiration to achieve buddhahood (see note 38) in order to help other beings and the engagement in the discipline by which that awakening can be realized. Ultimately, it denotes the direct understanding of the nature of reality. In short, bodhicitta is the unconditional intention to help all sentient beings become free of suffering. It is the complete abandonment of any sort of personal territory, both in one's relationships with others and in one's understanding of the world as it is. It begins with the development of love and compassion for others and matures into the full resolution to help them as much as possible.

When this basic compassionate aim is joined with direct nonconceptual knowledge of the nature of our experience, one becomes a bodhisattva. The term for this in Tibetan can be translated as "awakening warrior": awakening, because the process of purification and growth that will culminate in buddhahood has been set in motion; warrior, because of the courageous attitude that overcomes all obstacles and difficulties encountered in this way of life.

11. Serlingpa. This Buddhist master, who lived in Indonesia, held the transmission lineage of the special methods of cultivating bodhicitta known as mind training. He was the only one of Atisha's one hundred and fifty gurus to instruct him in this topic.

12. Drom-tön Rinpoche (1005–1064): The spiritual heir of Atisha. He received all Atisha's teachings and subsequently established the Kadampa school of Buddhism. Although a layman, he established the monastery of Ra-treng in 1056.

13. Kadampa: one of the first of the New Translation schools. This tradition emphasized strict observance of the monastic code, expertise in logic and scholarship, and diligence in basic virtuous practices as a basis for spiritual development. Not only did this tradition provide the initial training for such masters as Gampopa (Milarepa's spiritual heir and lineage holder of the Kagyu tradition), Kunga Gyaltsen (one of the founders of the Sakya school), and Tsongkapa (founder of the Gaden or Geluk tradition), but it also introduced the Lam-rim, or graded path, as a means of study and practice. In this ap-

proach, the student is led through a series of topics proceeding from the initial motivation of self-interest in liberation to the development of a totally altruistic concern to help others. This approach was subsequently utilized by all schools in Tibet.

14. Chekawa. This Kadampa teacher became a monk at the age of twenty-one and learned by heart the hundred volumes of the Buddha's teachings. Chekawa formulated Atisha's teachings of mind training into *The Seven Points of Mind Training*.

15. A translation and commentary on these verses may be found in *Kindness, Clarity, and Insight*, by H.H. the Fourteenth Dalai Lama Tenzin Gyatso (Snow Lion, 1984).

16. Bön. Generally regarded as preceding Buddhism in Tibet, this religion was greatly influenced by the advancement of Buddhism. In its present form, it is in many respects similar to Tibetan Buddhism, though with its own formulation and iconography.

17. Kagyupa. Literally meaning "the transmission of the teachings," this term refers to the Kagyupa schools established in Tibet by Marpa the Translator, his student Milarepa, and his student Gampopa (see note 30).

18. A traditional formula found at the beginning of many texts. The Sanskrit phrase means "Homage to gurus, buddhas, and bodhisattvas."

19. The two aims: the aim for oneself is to become free of suffering and confusion. This is realized through the understanding of emptiness (see notes 55–58) or ultimate bodhicitta. The second aim is to help others become free, and this is realized through compassion or relative bodhicitta.

20. Kongtrul here alludes to a group of eight bodhisattvas whose names are Manjushri, Avalokiteshvara, Vajrapani, Kshitigarbha, Vishkambi, Akashagarbha, and Samantabhadra.

21. Dharmakirti: the religious name of Serlingpa (see note 11).

22. Dharmarakshita. Initially a follower of the shravaka teachings of individual liberation (see notes 36 and 24), Dharmarakshita was moved by compassion when one of his associates fell very ill. The attending doctor said that only the flesh of a living person would cure the illness, but nothing could be

done since it would be impossible to obtain any. Dharmarakshita offered his own flesh, cutting out a piece of his thigh. Lacking the experiential understanding of emptiness, he suffered intensely, yet his compassion remained firm and he did not regret his action. The ill person ate the flesh and soon felt better. When Dharmarakshita heard this, he said that that was fine and he himself could now die peacefully. He was unable to rest because of the pain and it was almost dawn before he began to sleep. He dreamed of a white figure saying to him, "If you wish to attain enlightenment, you must do difficult things like this—very good." The figure in the dream then took some saliva from his mouth and rubbed it on the wound. The wound disappeared, leaving no trace. When Dharmarakshita awoke, he found his thigh completely healed, just as he had dreamed. An experiential understanding of emptiness arose, and he subsequently followed the mahayana path.

23. Yogin Maitreya. On one occasion when this Indian master was teaching, an onlooker threw a stone at a dog to drive it away. Maitreya cried out in pain and fell off his seat. Since the dog showed no sign of injury, everyone thought he was simply making a point. But when he showed people the bruise on his back, which corresponded exactly to the point where the dog had been struck, they realized that he had actually taken the pain of the dog onto himself.

24. The three kinds of students: a distinction made on the basis of motivation. The first kind is motivated by a wish to attain a better form of existence; the second by the wish to be free of the suffering of ego-based existence; the third by the wish to free all beings from suffering.

25. The names in romanized Tibetan are Khu.ston.brtson. 'grus.gyung.drung, rNgog.legs.pa'i.shes.rab, and 'Brom.-ston.rgyal.wa'i.'byung.gnas.

26. Although buddhahood (or full awakening) is undifferentiated, the expression of this experience in activity varies from individual to individual. The three families present different ways enlightenment may express itself, through form, speech, or mind. Shakyamuni Buddha and the bodhisattva Manjushri embody the form manifestation of awakening, Buddha Amitabha and Avalokiteshvara the speech, and Akshobya and Vaj-

rapani the mind. The three buddhas are the heads of the families, while the three bodhisattvas are the lords. The three students of Drom-tön who were regarded as emanations of these three bodhisattvas are Potowa, Chen-ngawa, and Puchungwa.

27. The Six Canonical Texts (gzhung.drug) of the Kadampa are: skyes.rabs, ched.du.brjod.pa'i.tshoms, byang.chub.spyod.-'jug, bslab.pa.kun.las.bstus.pa, byang.chub.sems.pa'i.sa, and nyan.thos.pa'i.sa. These texts present the previous lives of Shakyamuni Buddha, basic teachings on impermanence, suffering, and nonego, the development of bodhicitta, codes of conduct, and the descriptions of stages of spiritual development for shravakas and bodhisattvas.

The Key Instructions on the Four Truths (bden.bzhi'i.-gdams.ngag) are methods of contemplation based on the sutras (see note 34). They include such topics as the precious human existence, death and impermanence, action and result, the nature of cyclic existence, love, compassion, bodhicitta, mind training, and the six perfections.

The Pith Instructions (thig.le.bcu.drug.gi.man.ngag) are based on the tantras (see note 34) and deal with methods used to transform one's experience of the world.

28. Gelukpa (dge.lugs.pa): one of the four principal schools of the Tibetan tradition. It emphasized monastic discipline and a thorough grounding in logic and scriptural knowledge as a basis for contemplative practice. It originates with the founding of Gaden Monastery in 1409 by the great scholar and spiritual master Je Tsongkapa (1357–1419). Tsongkapa's life is an inspiring epic of unremitting determination and perseverance in penetrating the deepest teachings of Buddhism and of thorough and extensive scholarship, which continues to be singularly authoritative even today.

29. The Four Truths: the original formulation of Shakyamuni's teachings. The first truth is the truth of suffering: suffering is an inescapable element of our experience. The second is the truth of origin: disturbing emotions that cloud and confuse the mind are the source of suffering and frustration. The third is the truth of cessation: the causes of suffering as we know it can be eliminated. The fourth is the truth of the

path: The Noble Eightfold Path summarizes the way to live in
order to eliminate the sources of suffering.

30. Dakpo Kagyu: the collective name of a group of transmission lineages having a common source in Gampopa, or
Dakpo Lharje. Gampopa (1079–1153) first studied medicine
and became a doctor. When his wife died in an epidemic shortly
after the marriage, he lost all interest in conventional ways of
life. He became a monk and studied the Kadampa tradition
under several eminent masters, notably Jayulwa and several of
Drom-tön Rinpoche's students. He attained direct understanding of the dharma only when he studied with Milarepa, the
famous Kagyu poet-contemplative. Gampopa combined the
graded-path approach of the Kadampas with the mahamudra
teachings of the Kagyupas, causing these two rivers of teachings to become one.

Four of Gampopa's students founded separate transmissions
of the mahamudra teachings: Karma Kagyu, Tsalpa Kagyu,
Baram Kagyu, and Phagmo Kagyu. Subsequently, the Phagmo
Kagyu gave rise to eight more transmission lineages. All these
comprise the Dakpo Kagyu.

31. The four deities are Buddha Shakyamuni, Avalokiteshvara, Green Tara, and Acala.

32. The three containers are the three major collections of
scriptures: the vinaya, or monastic code; the sutras, which
explain the Four Truths; and the abhidharma teachings, which
describe the individual and the world in which he or she lives.

33. The three disciplines are morals and ethics, contemplative stability, and intelligence and wisdom.

34. The teachings of the mahayana, or great vehicle (see note
40), are divided into two groups, the sutras and the tantras.
The tradition of practice based on the sutras consists of cultivating qualities that will mature into the experience of
awakening: love, compassion, and bodhicitta, direct understanding of emptiness, the six perfections (generosity, mor-
ality, patience, diligence, stable contemplation, and wisdom),
and the four ways of attracting beings (providing what is
needed, speaking pleasantly, observing social customs, and en-
gaging in meaningful activity). In the tantra tradition, practice

consists of identifying with the result, that is, an expression of enlightenment, called a yidam. By identifying one's mind with the yidam, one comes to experience the world and oneself as expressions of enlightenment.

35. The three states of samsaric existence, which contain some experience of happiness: the human realm, the realm of asuras, or antigods, and the realm of gods. See notes 49 and 53.

36. Shravakas and pratyekabuddhas. These two kinds of spiritual attainment result from practice based on self-interest. The shravakas listen to the dharma and practice it in order to achieve their own freedom from suffering and frustration. With a basis of strong renunciation, their practice consists of observing the monastic code and developing a meditative composure through which they realize the lack of reality of the notion of individual self. With such an understanding, they overcome all disturbing emotions and are free of samsara. Pratyekabuddhas are similar, but their realization is deeper since it includes the understanding that subject and object are not independent entities. In both cases, however, they stop short of full buddhahood (see note 38); they have achieved only a state of rest from the world of suffering. In the course of time, they will respond to the inspiration of full awakening for the benefit of others and will set out on the mahayana path.

37. Nirvana, the transcendence of misery, always denotes freedom from samsaric existence. However, it sometimes refers to the attainment of shravakas and pratyekabuddhas, who do not realize full awakening (see notes 38 and 41).

38. Buddhahood, full awakening, is defined as the complete removal of the two veils or obscurations: the obscuration of disturbing emotions and the obscuration of conceptual knowledge. In comparison, the shravakas and pratyekabuddhas have eliminated only the obscuration of disturbing emotions, but the seeds of such emotions as well as the second obscuration remain. In the mahayana tradition, buddhahood is regarded as the end of a process of awakening that is brought about by the accumulation of merit and pristine awareness. Merit refers to a sense of wholesomeness or healthiness in our actions, speech, and thoughts. Through a compassionate attitude toward others, we develop warmth, openness, and helpfulness. In such

an environment, an understanding of the way we are, the way the world is, can develop. This kind of understanding is nonconceptual, immediate, and direct, and constitutes the development of pristine awareness.

When this kind of understanding is present, there is an awakening which is free from the limits of conceptual knowledge, beyond description, yet which embraces everything. This is called the dharmakaya of Buddha. Out of that understanding and through the force of merit accumulated, there arise the communication of the richness of enlightenment—the sambhogakaya of Buddha—and the actual manifestation of enlightenment in the world—the nirmanakaya of Buddha. (See note 67.)

39. The King of Mountains refers to Mount Meru, the center of the world according to traditional Buddhist cosmology. Mount Meru is generally identified with Mount Kailash, a large mountain in western Tibet.

40. Mahayana: the great vehicle. Although spiritual understanding is initially sought out of concern for one's own wellbeing, as the experience of practice matures, a change of heart may take place that leads to the motivation to come to full awakening in order to help others, i.e., bodhicitta (see note 10). The presence of bodhicitta as motivation characterizes the mahayana, which is known as the great vehicle because it carries all beings to freedom. It is contrasted with the hinayana, or small vehicle, which is based on the idea of attaining freedom only for oneself. The hinayana referred to in mahayana literature should not, however, be considered to refer to the southern schools of Buddhism in Thailand, Burma, and Sri Lanka.

41. Nonabiding nirvana: a synonym for full awakening or buddhahood. Because of his realization of emptiness, a buddha does not abide in samsaric existence, and because of his compassion and concern for others, he does not abide in the peace of the attainment of shravakas and pratyekabuddhas.

42. Shantideva (685–763). This Indian master was an adherent of the tradition of Profound Philosophy (see note 3) and is best known as the author of *Entering the Way of Awakening* (*Bodhicaryavatara*). This text is a long poem about bodhicitta,

what it is, and how it can be developed. Before composing this text, Shantideva was regarded by his fellow monks as a lazy, dim-witted person who just ate and slept. The monks decided to have a bit of fun and asked Shantideva to take his turn in delivering a discourse on the dharma at an annual festival sponsored by one of the monastery's patrons. Shantideva agreed, and when he took his seat, he asked his audience if they wished to hear something with which they were already familiar or an original exposition. Amid laughter, the monks called for an original exposition, and his response was *Entering the Way of Awakening.* As he started on the ninth chapter, which deals with ultimate bodhicitta, he started to rise from his seat and delivered the rest of his discourse from above the clouds.

43. Root guru. In the vajrayana, or tantric, tradition of Buddhism, the utmost importance is placed on the relationship between teacher and student. The vajrayana master is the source or root of inspiration for spiritual practice and the source of the teaching and training for that practice. More specifically, a root guru is one who confers the ability to practice vajrayana meditation through empowerment, the maturation of the experience of the student so that he or she can pursue such practice fruitfully. The guru also transmits the scriptures and explanations associated with a particular practice, thus providing the student with sound basis for meditation, and the actual instructions for practice by means of which the student is able to awaken.

44. Lotus-and-moon seat: an open lotus blossom on which rests the flat disk of the full moon. The lotus is an expression of unstained purity appearing amid the mud of samsara. The moon presents the refreshing calm of compassion after the burning heat of suffering, a image deriving from the hot days and cool nights of the North Indian plains.

45. Root and lineage gurus. (see note 43). The lineage gurus are the teachers who have carried the lineage of transmission of teaching from its source (Buddha Shakyamuni or Vajradhara Buddha) down to the present day. The transmission lineage is important; the origin of the teaching as well as its effectiveness are assured by the teachers of the lineage who have used and

practiced it themselves. Thus, students have grounds for confidence and inspiration that will help them to apply the teachings effectively.

46. The lineage prayer that Kongtrul wrote to accompany this commentary is in an appendix. It has been augmented by Kalu Rinpoche to include lineage holders since Jamgon Kongtrul.

47. The aperture of Brahma: the top of the head at a point eight finger-widths back from the hairline where the bones forming the skull meet.

48. Guru yoga. The term *yoga* in this context means "union," union with the mind of one's guru.

49. Samsara: The cycle of existence, so called because of the self-perpetuating nature of ego-based existence. Lack of awareness of one's own nature leads to the development of ego. The basic energies of mind are thus corrupted and become the source of confusion and emotional turmoil. Actions based on that confusion lead to a further sense of alienation and suffering, and the pattern of ego is strengthened. The antithesis of samsara is nirvana—the end of that lack of awareness and hence freedom from this endless and meaningless cycle.

50. The graded-path texts: see note 13. *The Jewel Ornament of Liberation* by sGam.po.pa, translated by H. V. Guenther, (Boston: Shambhala Publications, 1986), is a text of this genre.

51. Free and well favored. *Free* refers to freedom from eight forms of existence in which spiritual practice is virtually impossible: as a hell being, a preta, or an animal, in each of which the limitations posed by confusion and pain preclude spiritual concerns; as a god, where one is continually distracted by sensual pleasures; in an age when no buddha has appeared or in a primitive, uncivilized society; as someone with mental or physical incapacity or as someone who does not accept the validity of the dharma. *Well favored* refers to the conditions needed in order to practice. Five conditions derive from oneself: to be a human, to be born in a region where the dharma is asscessible, to have the use of all faculties, not to be swept away by the tide of one's own bad karma, and to have faith in the dharma. Five conditions derive from others: a buddha

must have appeared, he must have taught the dharma, the dharma must have lasted, there must be many who follow the dharma, and there must be people who support and maintain the practice of dharma.

52. *Karma* means "action," and, in Buddhist teaching, each act (physical, verbal, or mental) is a seed that develops into certain patterns of thought and experience. Thus, one's actions determine how one sees and experiences the world. Traditionally, it is said:

> To see what you've done, look at your body.
> To see what you'll be, look at your actions.

53. Six classes of beings: a traditional description of the possibilities of experience in samsara. The six classes are as follows:

1. Hell beings, whose existence is dominated by intense suffering in which the violent and extreme environment reflects the aggression that causes this kind of experience.
2. Pretas, or ghosts, whose existence is dominated by want, particularly for food and water. Their barren, lifeless environment reflects the greed that produces this kind of existence.
3. Animals, whose existence is dominated by fear of predators and being helplessly subject to their environment. Stupidity and insensitivity create this kind of experience.
4. Humans, whose experience consists of birth, illness, old age, and death as well as anxiety and ceaseless activity. The basic attachment that produces this experience manifests in the constant effort to maintain or improve one's immediate circumstances.
5. Asuras, or demigods, whose existence is dominated by fruitless and painful rivalry with the more powerful gods—a reflection of the basic jealousy that creates this experience.
6. Gods, whose relatively blissful existence in celestial paradises is terminated in fear and horror at

the vision of what their next existence will be.
Pride and arrogance are the causes of this form
of existence.

The six classes of beings are divided into two groups: the higher realms of gods, asuras, and humans; and the lower realms of animals, pretas, and hell beings.

54. The seven-branch prayer: a traditional format for mahayana practice. Paying homage counteracts pride; presenting offerings counteracts greed; acknowledging and confessing evil acts counteracts aggression; rejoicing in the good that others do counteracts jealousy; requesting spiritual teaching counteracts stupidity; asking the buddhas and teachers to remain present in the world counteracts the view of permanence; and dedicating virtue to the welfare of others leads to the attainment of full awakening. An example of this form of practice is included in an appendix.

55. Actual existence. For most people, objects of perception are experienced as independent actual entites. It is relatively straightforward to expose the inaccuracy of this kind of perception by logical analysis. However, even when there is some intellectual appreciation that objects of perception are not indivisible entities, depend on other factors for their appearance, and are not permanent, one still feels that the chair in the corner is a solid, real object existing independently of oneself or other factors. In this first instruction, one is encouraged to counteract this feeling and, instead, to cultivate some feeling for the phantomlike nature of experience, in which the objects of perception simply appear, empty of any kind of inherent existence, just like the images that arise in dreams.

56. Mind in itself. Application of the previous instructions necessarily leads to the understanding that phenomena are appearances arising in mind. The natural question is, "What is the nature of mind?" Mind, in Buddhist thought, does not denote any idea of self or pervasive metaphysical entity but refers simply to knowing, being aware. In the next instruction, this function of knowing is subjected to careful scrutiny to determine whether it is truly existent or not. In the subsequent instruction, attention is turned to the act of meditation itself.

In this way, one arrives at an appreciation of mind in itself, a term that refers to the nature of mind, which is at once empty, luminous, and unceasing.

57. Seven groups of consciousness. In Buddhist philosophy, the mind is viewed as a complex composed of eight kinds of consciousness. The first five are the consciousnesses associated with each of the five senses: sight, hearing, taste, smell, and touch. The sixth is the consciousness of thought and mental activity. The seventh is the consciousness of self, the felt sense of "I." It is referred to as the consciousness of the emotional mind since the felt sense of self is emotionally flavored and leads directly to the development of disturbing emotional states. The eighth consciousness is termed "the basis of everything," *alayavijñana*, and refers to a kind of consciousness that precedes ego in the sense that, while there are the predispositions toward samsara, the sense of self is not explicitly present. As long as the habits of ego-clinging are present, the other seven consciousnesses develop from alayavijñana.

58. The basis of everything, alaya. This term is used in reference to the eighth consciousness (see note 57) but here refers to mind as it is in itself when none of the confusion and constructions of samsara are present. When the process of samsara is halted and there is no further reinforcement of those tendencies, consciousness as the basis of everything (alayavijñana) subsides and mind as it is, the basis of everything (alaya), is known. In other editions of *The Seven Points of Mind Training*, this line reads:

> Rest in the essence of the path, the basis of everything.

The previous instructions have outlined a pattern of analysis that leads one to an understanding of the nature of mind. In order to cultivate this appreciation to the point that the disturbing and obscuring factors of ego-based habits subside and mind in itself is evident in its empty yet luminous presence, one must develop and foster the ability to let the mind rest in a clear, nondiscursive state, free from clinging or conceptual postulation. This state, when properly realized, is the basis of everything, alaya. When there is some lack of awareness, all the elaborations of consciousness and ego-based existence develop, but this basis is also the potential for buddhahood. It is buddha-nature, which will shine effortlessly like the sun once the clouds of confusion have been dispersed.

These four instructions present all the philosophy of Maitreya's teachings to Asanga. As it is said in Maitreya's teachings:

> After the awareness that there is nothing other than mind
> Comes the understanding that mind, too, is nothing itself.
> The intelligent know that these two understandings are not things.
> And then, not holding onto even this knowledge, they come to rest in the realm of totality.

These four lines correspond to the four instructions for meditation given in the text. Kongtrul gives a short commentary on these lines in his writings on philosophy:

> From time without beginning, mind, based on the incidental impurities of lack of awareness, arises as various appearances, which, if not investigated or examined, are like the bewildering appearances in dreams. When these appearances are examined, they do not exist as anything and are empty by virtue of what they are. Hence, all appearances are simply creations of mind. Consequently, the mode of being of the relatively real is that appearances, which are held to arise externally, have no inherent nature and are like the reflection of the moon in water.
>
> The mind that grasps, too, is not located anywhere externally or internally and does not exist concretely with a color or shape. From the continuity of egoclinging, which mistakes that which isn't (i.e., a self) for something which is, come the eight consciousnesses, which are like sky-flowers, empty from the beginning.
>
> Yet that which simply is, the pristine awareness or wisdom that is empty of fixation and grasping, is

present in all beings, from buddhas to sentient beings; it is the potential for buddhahood and is, by nature, totally luminous and has never been blemished by incidental impurities. This is the mode of being of the ultimately real.

When these two modes of being are properly recognized, one is to remain in that state of recognition. This is the point of *The Five Teachings of Maitreya*.

59. The idea here is that although experience of the world arises, when that experience is analyzed to determine what it is, nothing can be found to exist in fact. (See Kongtrul's comments in note 58.)

60. The translation "child of illusion" is due to Trungpa Rinpoche. Other teachers explain this line as "be a sorcerer." A sorcerer knows that the illusions that he creates through enchantments or spells are illusion. In the same way, one should know that the experiences that arise in life are simply appearances that arise in the mind and have no substantial existence.

61. The procedure for the development of bodhicitta consists of a sequence of contemplations, which may vary in order and subject matter depending on the tradition. However, the care and help one has received from one's parents is generally used as a basis for developing the experience of sincere warmth and appreciation.

The kindness of one's mother and the extent to which she cared for her child during pregnancy, birth, and infancy is, for some people, obscured by subsequent events in home and family life to the point that contemplation of one's parents as an example of kindness is initially difficult or impractical. In such cases, it may be more fruitful to begin this sequence with contemplation on a close friend, teacher, or other individual whose help and kindness are appreciated.

Alternatively, one may find that imagining that one *never* had a mother will bring about a different appreciation of one's relationship.

In any case, since development of a basis of some kind of

experience of warmth toward all sentient beings is essential for the fruitful practice of taking and sending, it is worthwhile exploring all aspects of these contemplations to find those methods which one is able to use effectively.

62. Source of suffering: emotional states of mind and the actions that develop from them. The term for emotion in Tibetan carries the idea of disturbance and dullness, implying that emotions cloud and confuse the mind. Thus, actions that develop from such feelings are generally at odds with the situation and create more probems. The mental patterns laid down in thinking and acting in this way create the potential for further confusion and disturbance, and hence more suffering.

63. Gyal-se Tokme (1295–1369): a Kadampa teacher famed for his practice of bodhicitta. He was probably the first to write a commentary on *The Seven Points*, and all subsequent works refer to him.

64. Carrying practice into everyday life. The Tibetan idiom literally means "to carry [one's practice] to the [spiritual] path"—in other words, to make one's practice effective. The criteria of effectiveness in Buddhist training are not simply how well one can sit in meditation or how well one can focus the mind, but how thoroughly the understanding one develops through meditation permeates one's life and one's relationships with others, how present it is in everyday activity, and to what extent it is reflected in one's behavior.

65. God or demon. In the course of awakening to the nature of the world, there is a natural increase in one's sensitivity and perception of the many influences that shape and determine one's personality and environment. These influences may be experienced as an intangible presence or feeling associated with a certain locality, as disturbances in physical or mental well-being, or as images and patterns encountered in dreams, at the point of sleep, or in actual life. These experiences may be heavenly (pleasurable and enjoyable) or demonic (horrific and terrifying). The approach in mind training to such disturbances is to accept the situation as it is and use it, however positively or negatively flavored, as a stimulus to wakefulness and an opportunity to express compassion.

66. The reader is referred to the earlier discussion on ultimate bodhicitta. The point of view here is that all that we have to deal with is our experience of the world, and that the world is a world of experience rather than an external entity that exists independently of us. Thus, *how* we perceive determines *what* we experience. We tend to perceive the world as being real, independent, and so on, but this view cannot be maintained in the light of analysis. We come to the conclusion that all our experience is just that—the arising of experiences, some fixed and solid, such as our perception of the world, others fleeting and intangible, such as our thoughts and ideas.

67. The four kayas. Buddhahood is described in terms of four kayas (literally "bodies") or four aspects of being. The first is dharmakaya, or being as truth. It is like space, without beginning or end, total simplicity, beyond any logical determination, and free of all limitations or obscurations. The second is sambhogakaya, or being as full of qualities. Its domain is the pure realm of natural well-being. It arises in a variety of forms as the expression of compassion and communicates awakening as transcending awareness to high-level bodhisattvas. The third is nirmanakaya, or being as expression. Its domain is the world of the experience of sentient beings, and it reveals awakening in many different ways that inspire beings to seek freedom from ego-oriented existence. The fourth is svabhavikakaya, or being as it is. It is not so much a fourth kaya as it is a way of expressing the inseparability of the preceding three. Although these four aspects of being are realized in their entirety only when all lack of awareness and obscurations have been eliminated, they are present in all experience. In his commentary, Kongtrul points out those aspects of experience which correspond to the four kayas.

68. Torma: a kind of offering or gift whose significance is explained as that which has power and capability. *Power* indicates the power of overcoming the deadening effect of ego, and *capability* indicates the ability to overcome the four obsessions (obsession with emotions, mortality, entertainment, and physical existence). In presenting torma to gods and demons, one acknowledges these forces and influences in one's experi-

ence and comes to terms with them. In presenting torma to dakinis and protectors (see note 69), one nourishes the presence of awakened activity in one's experience.

A typical ceremony for this sort of offering will include a consecration of the physical torma (usually a cake or pastry fashioned and decorated according to the particular purpose of the ceremony) in order to appreciate the richness and possibilities of experience and its presentation to the recipients. Such practices function simultaneously on several levels, as illustrated by the following excerpt from a collection of prayers of the Karma Kagyu tradition:

> In the bowl formed by the universe of world
>   systems
> Rests the torma of the four elements (earth, water,
>   fire, and wind).
> I offer it to the four guardian kings and the throng
>   of wrathful gods.
> Bless me with the full performance of your work
>   for me.
>
> In the bowl formed by my own skin
> Rests the torma of my flesh, blood, and bones.
> I offer it to the vast host of protectors of the
>   dharma.
> Bless me with a life that shines like the sun and
>   moon.
>
> In the bowl formed by the various appearances
>   that arise in mind
> Rests the torma of clear mindfulness and awareness.
> I offer it to the all-pervading dharmakaya.
> Bless me with the five pristine wisdoms.

69. Dakinis and protectors: expressions of awakened activity. The former are female figures who embody compassion and emptiness and, in particular, present the playfulness of mind in the space of total simplicity. Hence the name *dakini*, which means "she who travels in the sky." Protectors are generally wrathful expressions of bodhisattvas who have undertaken to assist practitioners by clearing away disruptive forces

through the four kinds of activity—pacifying, enriching, magnetizing, and destroying.

70. Mandala. In this context, *mandala* refers to the practice of offering the whole universe with all its richness and beauty to one's guru, the buddhas, etc. In this practice, grains of rice are arranged on a disc of copper or silver in a pattern derived from traditional Buddhist cosmology.

71. Hope can be understood as ego's attempt to establish its own priorities, while fear is ego's reaction to threats to its survival. The two patterns continue to arise until ego-clinging is completely removed.

72. Mantras and dharanis: formulæ for recitation associated with particular buddhas, bodhisattvas, and other figures. A dharani is essentially a very concise prayer that fosters recollection of bodhicitta and guards against its neglect. Mantras guard the mind from nondharmic attitudes.

73. The seven-point posture. The legs are crossed in vajra position; the right hand is placed on the left, and both rest with thumbs touching at the level of the navel; the back is held straight; the lips and teeth are closed but not clenched, and the tongue is placed against the palate; the arms are bent and held slightly out from the body; the chin is drawn in toward the throat; and the eyes rest without straining on a point about eight finger-widths in front of the nose.

74. Ordination. These three levels of ordination correspond to the three approaches to practice: hinayana, mahayana, and vajrayana. In the first, emphasis is placed on restraint, non-aggression, and a simple, straightforward way of life that does not hurt or cause harm to others. The ordination of individual liberation is concerned principally with physical and verbal conduct. There are several types of ordination at this level, from fully ordained monk or nun to a layperson who observes possibly only one vow. However, the essence of the ordination is found in the four vows not to kill, not to steal, not to lie, and not to engage in inappropriate sexual relationships. In the mahayana, the emphasis is on compassion and bodhicitta. The corresponding ordination, the bodhisattva vow, focuses on one's relationship with others—that is, one's aspiration to

buddhahood in order to help all beings. This ordination is more a vow of conscience and is violated even by the decision never to help a certain individual or by a sense of despair or futility in one's intention to help others by attaining buddhahood. At the vajrayana level, one identifies directly with awakened mind. This form of practice requires a pure vision of the world and a commitment to maintain that vision.

75. The kinds of actions Kongtrul cites here would be considered scandalous in Tibetan society. Slashing trees, for instance, would indicate complète disregard for local deities residing in groves and woods. Polluting bodies of water by urinating in them would indicate a similar disregard for nagas. In Western societies, this sort of exhibitionism might take the form of highly unconventional dress or a blatant lack of manners or personal hygiene.

76. The Tibetan text refers to a dzo and an ox. The dzo is a cross between a yak and a cow and has much greater carrying capacity than an ox.

77. Revealed teachings or treasure teachings. In the course of the history of Buddhism, new formulations of the Buddha's teachings and different techniques of practice have been revealed by certain teachers. In Tibet, such revealed works were called "treasures" hidden by Guru Padmasambhava for the benefit of future generations.

78. Monks could expect sizable offerings and donations when they performed ceremonies for healing sick people or conducted funeral ceremonies.

79. Ra-treng (Rwa.sgreng): the monastery founded by Drom-tön Rinpoche in 1056.

80. The word *yidam* means "that to which the mind is bound." Generally, it is a vajrayana term for an expression of enlightened mind that is used in meditation (see note 34). Here, however, the advice means to invoke the compassion and intelligence that develop through mind training.

81. Potowa: a student of Drom-tön Rinpoche and a holder of the Kadampa lineage.

82. Tsang-tsen is the name of a protective deity associated

with the Nyingma tradition. He has a reputation of being extremely sensitive and easily irritated.

83. Gyal-se Rinpoche: Gyal-se Tokme. See note 63.

84. *The Stages of the Awakening Warrior*: a series of short texts on mind training that can be found in *Blo.sbyong.brgya.rtsa* (A Hundred Teachings on Mind Training), a collection by dKon.mchog.rgyal.mtsan published in Dharamsala, India.

85. These teachings were given by Serlingpa to Atisha before he left for Tibet.

86. Despite the metaphorical language, there is no suggestion of suppression of emotions in these methods. The proper use of these techniques does not result in the dangerous effects of simply suppressing emotions. Guidance by a qualified teacher is necessary to understand how to practice properly.

87. Kunga Nyingpo. Better known as Taranatha, this great scholar and contemplative lived at the end of the sixteenth century and was the last lineage holder of the Jonangpa tradition.

Appendices

THE SEVEN POINTS
OF MIND TRAINING

The Preliminaries, Which Teach the Support for Dharma

First, train in the preliminaries.

The Actual Practice: Training in Bodhicitta

ULTIMATE BODHICITTA
Regard all phenomena as dreams.
Examine the nature of unborn awareness.
Even the remedy is freed to subside naturally.
Rest in the nature of all, the basis of everything.
In postmeditation practice, be a child of illusion.

RELATIVE BODHICITTA
Train in taking and sending alternately.
Put them on the breath.
Three objects, three poisons, three seeds of virtue.
Use sayings to train in all forms of activity.
Begin the sequence of exchange with yourself.

*The Transformation of Adverse Conditions
into the Path of Awakening*

When evil fills the world and its inhabitants,
Change adverse conditions into the path of awakening.

RELATIVE BODHICITTA
Drive all blame into one.
Be grateful to everyone.

ULTIMATE BODHICITTA
To see confusion as the four kayas,
The protection of emptiness is insurpassable.

SPECIAL PRACTICES
The four applications are the best method.
In order to take unexpected conditions as the path,
Immediately join whatever you meet with meditation.

The Utilization of the Practice in One's Whole Life

WHAT TO DO DURING ONE'S LIFE
A summary of the essential instructions:
Train in the five forces.

WHAT TO DO AT DEATH
The mahayana instructions for how to die
Are the five forces. How you act is important.

The Extent of Proficiency in Mind Training

All dharma has a single purpose.
Of the two judges, rely on the principal one.
Always have the support of a joyful mind.
You are proficient if you can practice even when
    distracted.

Commitments of Mind Training

Always practice the three general principles.
Change your attitude, but remain natural.
Do not talk about weak points.
Don't think about the affairs of others.
Work on the stronger disturbing emotions first.
Give up all hope for results.
Give up poisonous food.
Don't rely on consistency.
Don't be excited by cutting remarks.
Don't wait in ambush.

Don't make things painful.
Don't put the horse's load on a pony.
Don't aim to win.
Don't revert to magic.
Don't reduce a god to a demon.
Don't seek pain as a component of happiness.

Guidelines for Mind Training

All active meditation is done in one way.
All corrections are made in one way.
At the beginning and at the end,
Two things to be done.
Whichever of two occurs, be patient.
Observe these two, even at the risk of your life.
Learn the three difficult points.
Take up the three primary resources.
Don't allow three things to weaken.
Make the three inseparable.
Train in all areas without partiality.
Overall deep and pervasive proficiency is important.
Always meditate on volatile points.
Don't depend on external conditions.
This time, practice the important points.
Don't make mistakes.
Don't fluctuate.
Train wholeheartedly.
Find freedom through both examination and
    investigation.
Don't make a fuss.
Don't be caught up in irritation.
Don't be temperamental.
Don't expect thanks.

Concluding Verses

This quintessential elixir of instruction,
Which changes the five kinds of degeneration

Into the way of awakening,
Is a transmission from Serlingpa.
The awakening of the karmic energy of previous
    training
Aroused intense interest in me.
Therefore, I ignored suffering and criticism
And sought instruction for subduing ego-clinging.
Now, when I die, I'll regret nothing.

THE ROOT TEXT OF THE SEVEN POINTS OF TRAINING THE MIND

Translated by the Nālandā Translation Committee under the direction of Vidyādhara the Venerable Chögyam Trungpa, Rinpoche

ONE: *The Preliminaries, Which Are a Basis for Dharma Practice*
First, train in the preliminaries.
TWO: *The Main Practice, Which Is Training in Bodhichitta*
[ULTIMATE AND RELATIVE BODHICHITTA]
[ULTIMATE BODHICHITTA SLOGANS]
Regard all dharmas as dreams.
Examine the nature of unborn awareness.
Self-liberate even the antidote.
Rest in the nature of alaya, the essence.
In postmeditation, be a child of illusion.
[RELATIVE BODHICHITTA SLOGANS]
Sending and taking should be practiced alternately.
These two should ride the breath.
Three objects, three poisons, and three seeds of virtue.
In all activities, train with slogans.
Begin the sequence of sending and taking with
    yourself.

THREE: *Transformation of Bad Circumstances into the Path of Enlightenment*
[POINT THREE AND THE PARAMITA OF PATIENCE]
> When the world is filled with evil,
>> transform all mishaps into the path of bodhi.
> Drive all blames into one.
> Be grateful to everyone.
> Seeing confusion as the four kayas
>> is unsurpassable shunyata protection.
> Four practices are the best of methods.
> Whatever you meet unexpectedly, join with
>> meditation.

FOUR: *Showing the Utilization of Practice in One's Whole Life*
[POINT FOUR AND THE PARAMITA OF EXERTION]
> Practice the five strengths,
> The condensed heart instructions.
> The mahayana instruction for ejection of
>> consciousness at death
> Is the five strengths: how you conduct yourself is
>> important.

FIVE: *Evaluation of Mind Training*
[POINT FIVE AND THE PARAMITA OF MEDITATION]
> All dharma agrees at one point.
> Of the two witnesses, hold the principal one.
> Always maintain only a joyful mind.
> If you can practice even when distracted, you are well
>> trained.

SIX: *Disciplines of Mind Training*
[POINT SIX AND PRAJNAPARAMITA]
> Always abide by the three basic principles.
> Change your attitude, but remain natural.

SEVEN: *Guidelines of Mind Training*
[POINT SEVEN AND POSTMEDITATION]

All activities should be done with one intention.
Correct all wrongs with one intention.
Two activities: one at the beginning, one at the end.
Whichever of the two occurs, be patient.
Observe these two, even at the risk of your life.
Train in the three difficulties.
Take on the three principal causes.
Pay heed that the three never wane.
Keep the three inseparable.
Train without bias in all areas.
It is crucial always to do this pervasively and
    wholeheartedly.
Always meditate on whatever provokes resentment.
Don't be swayed by external circumstances.
This time, practice the main points.
Don't misinterpret.
Don't vacillate.
Don't talk about injured limbs.
Don't ponder others.
Work with the greatest defilements first.
Abandon any hope of fruition.
Abandon poisonous food.
Don't be so predictable.
Don't malign others.
Don't wait in ambush.
Don't bring things to a painful point.
Don't transfer the ox's load to the cow.
Don't try to be the fastest.
Don't act with a twist.
Don't make gods into demons.
Don't seek others' pain as the limbs of your own
    happiness.

Train wholeheartedly.
Liberate yourself by examining and analyzing.
Don't wallow in self-pity.
Don't be jealous.
Don't be frivolous.
Don't expect applause.

When the five dark ages occur,
This is the way to transform them into the path of bodhi.
This is the essence of the amrita of the oral instructions,
Which were handed down from the tradition of the sage of
    Suvarnadvipa.

Having awakened the karma of previous training
And being urged on by intense dedication,
I disregarded misfortune and slander
And received oral instruction on taming ego-fixation.
Now, even at death, I will have no regrets.

[These two verses are the concluding comments of Geshe Chekawa Yeshe Dorje, the author of *The Root Text of the Seven Points
of Training the Mind.*]

SOOTHING THE PAIN OF FAITH
A PRAYER TO THE MIND-TRAINING
LINEAGE

THIS PRAYER was composed by Lodru Taye (Jamgon Kongtrul) to be included with the written commentary on mind training. Additions to the lineage were made by Kalu Rinpoche.

All the lineages of the mind training transmission share a common genesis in Buddha Shakyamuni, the Indian masters including Atisha, and the early Kadampa teachers. Different lines of transmission begin to emerge in the eleventh and twelfth centuries. Kongtrul follows the Kadampa lineage up to Tokme Zangpo, who authored the first commentary on Chekawa's *Seven Points*. By this time there were many systems of mind training. Shakya Chokden, a teacher of the Sakya tradition, received some sixty different teachings from Shon-nu Lodru. With Kunga Chokdrup, this line of transmission enters the Jonangpa school and continues as part of the Shangpa transmission after Taranatha's time. The Shangpa transmission, in turn, was carried by teachers of several different schools: Tsewang Norbu, a Nyingma master; Trin-le Shingta, a Drukpa Kagyu master; Situ Tenpa Nyinje of the Karma Kagyu tradition; and others. Kongtrul (Lodru Taye) received these teachings from Shenpen Ozer, a Shangpa lineage holder, though he undoubtedly received them from other teachers, too. After Kongtrul, the line of transmission, as augmented by Kalu

Rinpoche, follows the Karma Kagyu and Shangpa lineage holders in eastern Tibet.

Glorious root guru, the precious one,
Sitting above my head on a lotus-and-moon seat,
With your great kindness, please take care of me.
Grant the mastery of enlightened form, speech, and
    mind.

I pray to Shakyamuni and his regent Maitreya,
To the noble Asanga and the learned Vasubandhu,
To the two Sena and Gunamitra, and to Simhabhadra.
Bless me with the full development of love,
    compassion, and bodhicitta,
And the ability to dismiss and dispel.*

I pray to Gang-pel and the greater and lesser Kusali,
To Dharmakirti and lord Atisha,
To Drom-tön, Potowa, and Sharawa,
And to the contemplative Chekawa.
Bless me with the full development of love,
    compassion, and bodhicitta,
And the ability to dismiss and dispel.

I pray to Chilbupa and guru Ozer,
To Lha-ding, Jang-chub Bum, and Kun-gyaltsen,
To Yonten-pal and the great pandit Dewa-pal,
And to Shon-nu, who proclaimed the four teachings.
Bless me with the full development of love,
    compassion, and bodhicitta,
And the ability to dismiss and dispel.

I pray to the bodhisattva Sonam Trakpa,
To Tok-me Zangpo, Yonten Lodru, and
    Shon-nu Lodru,

---

*Dismiss and dispel. In his writings, Kongtrul explains *dismiss* as
the dismissal of ego-clinging and *dispel* as the dispelling of disturbing
emotions.

To the great pandit Shakya Chokden,
And to Kunga Chokdrup and Jetsun Drolchok.
Bless me with the full development of love,
    compassion, and bodhicitta,
And the ability to dismiss and dispel.

I pray to Lung-rik Gyatso and all-knowing Taranatha,
To the two regents Rinchen Gyatso and Yeshe Gyatso,
To the contemplative Yonten Gon, to Gonpo Paljor,
Gonpo Trakpa, and to Gonpo Namgyal.
Bless me with the full development of love,
    compassion, and bodhicitta,
And the ability to dismiss and dispel.

I pray to Tsewang Norbu and Trin-le Shingta,
To Situ Tenpa Nyinje and the siddha Lodru,
To Karma Lhatong, Shenpen Ozer, and Lodru Taye.
Bless me with the full development of love,
    compassion, and bodhicitta,
And the ability to dismiss and dispel.

I pray to Kachab Dorje and Shiwa Nyingpo,
To Padma Wangchuk and Khyentse Ozer,
To Norbu Dondrub, whose experience and
    understanding were complete,
And to all the root and lineage gurus.
Bless me with the full development of love,
    compassion, and bodhicitta,
And the ability to dismiss and dispel.

In your form is united the compassion of Buddha and
    his sons.
You are the incomparable lord of dharma with whom
    any relationship is meaningful.
My root guru, you embody the life-breath of this
    lineage.
I pray to you from the depths of my heart.
Bless me with the full development of love,

compassion, and bodhicitta,
And the ability to dismiss and dispel.

Revulsion and renunciation form the foundation.
Supreme pure bodhicitta in its two aspects
Is the secret for never veering from the mahayana path.
Grant your blessings that bodhicitta may arise,
Be stabilized, and grow in strength.

When the confusion of the eight concerns* has been
thrown over,
Ego-clinging completely severed,
And genuine concern for others thoroughly developed,
Whatever appears can be experienced as an aid on the
path of awakening.
Grant your blessings that mind training may be
complete.

With the direct understanding that what is ultimate
has no origin, cessation, or duration, is emptiness,
Yet what is present arises from dependence and
coincidence like an enchantment,
May I come to see everything and work naturally for
the welfare of limitless beings
As long as samsara exists.

* The eight concerns: gain and loss, happiness and suffering, fame
and notoriety, praise and blame.

THE SEVEN-BRANCH PRAYER

With complete faith I bow
To all the victorious ones and their sons
Who abide in the ten directions and three times.

I offer flowers, incense, light,
Perfume, food, music, and many other things,
Both in substance and with my imagination.
I ask the noble assemblage to accept them.

I confess all evil actions that I have done,
Influenced by the defilements,
From time without beginning until now:
The five that ripen immediately,
The ten nonvirtuous acts, and many others.

I rejoice in the merit of whatever virtue
Shravakas, pratyekabuddhas,
Bodhisattvas, and ordinary people
Gather throughout the three times.

I pray for the wheel of the dharma to be turned,
The teachings of the mahayana and hinayana,
In ways suitable for the different aptitudes
And motivations present in sentient beings.

I ask the buddhas not to pass into nirvana,
But, with great compassion and
Until samsara is completely empty,
To look after all sentient beings
Who drown in this ocean of sorrow.

May whatever merit I have accumulated
Become a seed for the enlightenment of all beings.
Without delay, may I become
A splendid leader for sentient beings.